What He Can't Tell You . . .

And Needs to Say

What
He Can't
Tell You . . .

And Needs to Say

Brenda Shoshanna, Ph.D.

A Perigee Book

Perigee Books
Published by The Berkley Publishing Group
A division of Penguin Putnam Inc.
375 Hudson Street
New York, New York 10014

First edition: June 2001

Published simultaneously in Canada.

The Penguin Putnam Inc. World Wide Web site address is
www.penguinputnam.com

Library of Congress Cataloging-in-Publication Data

Shoshanna, Brenda.
What he can't tell you . . . and needs to say / Brenda Shoshanna.
    p. cm.
Includes index.
ISBN 0-399-52677-3
   1. Men—Psychology. 2. Interpersonal communication. 3. Man-
woman relationships.
 I. Title.
HQ1090 .S533 2001
155.3'32—dc21

                                               00-045273

Printed in the United States of America

10 9 8 7 6 5 4 3 2 1

*This book is dedicated to
all the wonderful men who are in it and so
generously shared their time and hearts.*

CONTENTS

ACKNOWLEDGMENTS

I wish to offer special thanks and acknowledgments to my wonderful agent, Noah Lukeman, who assisted me in all aspects of this book's construction and to my wonderful editor, Sheila Curry Oakes, whose encouragement and belief in my work is a long-standing source of warm support. In addition, I wish to thank Adam Lukeman, my web designer and webmaster for his continual creative input and caring, and all of my family—Melissa, Abram, Josh, Yana, Daniel, Leah, Gerry, Zöe, Remy, Jacob—and others whose support and love assist me so much in going on.

INTRODUCTION

It seems the number one complaint women have about their boyfriends, spouses, male friends and family members is that men don't talk. "I don't know what he's thinking," a woman will say to her friend or therapist. "He never tells me what is going on with him. How can I get him to open up?" While the strong, silent type might be fascinating in the beginning, as the relationship goes on, he falls short. The woman finds herself lonely, unable to work through the differences between them. Although the women may not realize it, the men find themselves lonely as well.

What these women don't understand is that the men are dying to open up and tell what's going on. Many of them are silenced by the roles they are forced to play, the lessons they've learned from their own families, or past relationships. Because men have relegated themselves to hiding behind a mask, or becoming stuck in a limited role that does not express all of who they are, their search for fulfillment is often fruitless. Many find themselves alienated, lacking true identity and constantly searching for happiness and meaning. The good news, however, is that this state of affairs can be remedied rather simply.

Firstly, a man must have permission to speak out honestly about who he is. A man needs to accept and express the full range of his being in order to live a satisfying life.

I have had the privilege of hearing men speak—candidly and openly—about their fears, pain and doubts about themselves as partners, lovers, fathers and friends. In the process I have learned what it is that helps a man feel free to open up and talk. Their candor provides great insight into the lives men lead today in this world of shifting values, that is sadly devoid of Heroes.

This book, in giving men a chance to speak, will help reveal what keeps us from knowing and loving the men we live with. It reveals to men what prevents them from knowing and loving themselves. When we can all understand the forces that operate on a man's heart and behavior, we can better understand how to meet those forces, resolve conflict and open the door for men to be all they are meant to be. As that happens it is easy to realize that each man contains everything—the Hero, Warrior, Wise Man, Lover and Fool.

All men long for role models who express the biggest and best a man can be. When a man can speak his mind and be accepted, he is on the way to living to the fullest extent of who he is.

Listen carefully to what these men are saying, and what it is that allowed them to open up and speak. Then you will be able to open your ears and heart to the man in your life so that he is able to tell you what he needs to say to you.

This book will take you on a journey of discovery. In order to assist this discovery process, each chapter contains a quiz called The Personal Inventory, and Touchstones to Remember. The Personal Inventory will allow you to score the man in your life on questions relating to that chapter. The answers will you give you an overall picture of where he fits, what his needs, strengths, and fears are. The Touchstones to Remember at the end of each chapter give specific guidance and insights for the different kinds of men on the subject matter covered.

I hope that men and women readers will discover much about themselves in this book. I also hope that it will help to bridge the communication gap that seems to exist between men and women.

I may be contacted via web page (*BrendaShoshanna.com*) or e-mail (*topspeaker@yahoo.com*). Workshops, speaking engagements, and personal consultations are available.

—Brenda Shoshanna, Ph.D

What He Can't Tell You . . .

And Needs to Say

ONE

Who Is He?

When we meet anyone for the first time, we immediately want to know who he is, where's he from, what's his profession, is he religious, how will he act? What we really want to know is, is he like me? What can I expect? Is this a person to be trusted? Is he my kind? There's an instinctive desire to place him in a category so we can feel as if he is familiar, and be at ease. We do this with ourselves as well, searching for ways to define ourselves that fit a preconceived mold. As Ralph Waldo Emerson puts it, "We come to wear one cut of face and figure, to acquire by degrees the gentlest asinine expression. But with consistency a great soul has nothing to do."

Living without answering the question "Who am I?" places us in a prison without bars. It limits ourselves and others enormously. Whatever answer we offer can only be a small fragment of the truth. Who a man is today, he may not be tomorrow. The essence of all life is growth and change. The history of nations as well as people is filled with developments that amaze us all.

Throughout all history the question of *Who am I* has challenged philosophers, psychologists, truth seekers, and thinkers of all kinds. Socrates, the father of philosophy, summed up his years of thought with the injunction to "Know thyself." Without an answer to this precious question, a human being is prey to confusion, deceit, and the great sorrow of living a life that is unreal, and cannot ultimately bring satisfaction or fulfillment to himself or others. In Zen practice one is told to "Find the true man of no rank." In other words, let go of the false self and live from one's original nature, which, it is taught, alone has the capacity to bring joy and richness to one's life.

Although these concepts may sound esoteric, they are based upon the simple truth that, unless a life is based upon the bedrock of true identity, an individual can fall prey to compulsions and misfortunes. He will waver between devotion to and rebellion against the significant people in his life. The love he gives and receives will be conditional, given one moment and taken away the next.

From the Eastern point of view, man is subject to his *karma*, or the accumulated effect of his words, thoughts and deeds. This is based upon the principle of cause and effect, which says that the seeds we plant, will inevitably bear fruit when conditions appear to make them grow. A seed planted in the right soil, watered regularly, with the right amount of sun must yield a certain kind of flower. The seed of an iris will never produce a rose. The same is true for our thoughts, words and deeds, from this life and possibly other lifetimes as well. When the right people, places and situations arise, karmic seeds we have planted will burst into bloom. A life which may have been full of happiness and ease may suddenly come upon difficult times, filled with obstacles and painful situations. A person may then change drastically.

These changes are not considered to be accidental, but inevitable, the ripening of a man's karma, the effect of previous thoughts, words and deeds. Now we may ask again, who is he? A wealthy man has suddenly turned poor, the most popular man, is now unwanted. What's going on? Is he the same person? Is he being punished by God? What has he done to cause his misery?

Defining a Person

Do we define a person by their situation in life? Or do we look deeper and define them by the manner in which they react and respond to the changes life brings? So many times we hear married couples say that the mate is not the same person he or she was when they met. Of course they aren't. How can they be? The changes of daily life are inexorable. They alter us, whether we want them to or not.

Who a person is will be discovered by how they handle whatever life brings. Challenges and difficult situations become a means of revealing what's truly inside. Does a man become stronger, wiser, or more compassionate when faced with difficulty? He may not have control over the situations which arise, but does have choice and control over the ways in which he responds, what he learns, and how he grows. Does he become bitter, hostile and hopeless, making life miserable for everyone, or does he develop new strength and meaning from within?

In this sense, life is a constant unfolding. The answer to the question "Who is he?" is never complete. Tomorrow something new can happen and he may discover new aspects of himself. This is the essence of hope. While change can be painful, if it did not occur, nothing could stretch or grow.

In trying to understand who a man is, rather than place

him in a category, it is crucial to realize that each person contains all possibilities. Whatever is expressed in the human experience is part of our collective unconscious. That which we praise or condemn in another, is also somewhere deep within ourselves. At different times in our lives, different parts of ourselves will be revealed. The Warrior, Healer, Lover, Wise Man, are all buried inside, waiting to be called forth.

Some roles are lived out, others demand to be heard sooner or later. If we want to know more about who we are, what we truly treasure and resonate with, we can look at the people we surround ourselves with. Take a good look at your mate, children, friends, clients, students. Each is expressing something within you. Take a look at the ones you love and also the ones you reject. If someone is part of your life on an ongoing basis, realize they are there for a reason. You are looking in the mirror at a part of yourself.

There is a wonderful exercise which helps make this real. If you are having difficulty with some person in your life, write a little scene based upon what goes on between the two of you. Gather some friends to be actors in it. Get together and play this scene out in your living room. You play the role of your adversary. Get someone else to play the part of you. Become your adversary completely in the scene. By the time the scene has been played out, you will have a much greater understanding of this person's feelings and needs. They will no longer seem like an adversary, but just another part of you. Sympathy and understanding will develop. Natural solutions to the problem between you will arise.

Becoming Whole

A big step in answering the question of "Who is he," or "Who am I," is embarking on the process of becoming whole.

This means learning to openly greet, know, and accept all aspects of the human experience, putting an end to judgment and condemnation, both of others, and of ourselves. There may be parts of ourselves and others that need growth. These are the parts that want love most of all. Nothing grows when it is battered. Fear, guilt and rejection are the surest way to keep the mess alive.

Some fortunate individuals come to an experience of Oneness with all of creation. This brings deep inner changes and is greatly valuable if integrated into the tapestry of their entire life. Even with these peak experiences, there will still be daily confusion and challenges. We are constantly being tested and refined in the daily furnace of our lives. There is no end to the discovery and growth possible.

Who we are is the infinite possibility for renewal and love. Living a wide awake life, no matter what age or circumstance allows these possibilities to be realized.

TWO

Male Identity
(How It Is Formed)

"Insufficiency of being causes him to play roles."
—Sartre

Today the roles of men—husband, lover and father—are going through so many changes that men need to find out who they are, where they are going, and what they truly need. They have a craving to understand themselves in relationships, and they want others to understand them too.

The common myth is that men don't like to talk about personal matters. More than a myth, this is an injunction society places upon men—real men don't share their feelings, give their power away, or need to find out who they truly are. Society has provided different images for men, and most live their lives through them. They come to define themselves as "the macho man," "good provider," "great lover" or "husband," "devoted son," "caring father." Uncertain about who they really are, and what is truly demanded of them, most put great energy into protecting their fragile sense of identity, formed, in great measure, by society's image and demands. Many pay for this dearly.

Neither men nor women have any real idea of who a man is—what his basic needs, drives, fantasies and unconscious compulsions are—what it is that really makes him happy. There is little understanding of what constitutes male identity, or how it is formed. We assume all men have the same heroes and aspirations, feel the same way about women and relationships. Nothing could be further from the truth.

To understand men in today's society we will begin by looking at how male identity is formed and what is needed to sustain and develop one's true self. (The common wisdom has it that, when all goes well, men identify with their fathers, taking upon themselves their behaviors, dreams and character traits. The father is enhanced and acknowledged by this identification and the son receives value and praise in his father's eyes.)

According to Dr. Robert Jay Berk, Freudian psychoanalyst and training analyst, the successful resolution of the Oedipal struggle (in which the son competes with his father for the mother) comes when the son gives up the mother as his primary love object and identifies with the father. The boy loses the mother, gains the father and basically gains himself. This is the basis of all future friendships between men, and also the basis of man's ability to find a love object of his own one day.

Needless to say, many young men do not have father figures to identity with, and even when they do, often choose to reject them. They may observe behaviors in their fathers which are unacceptable to them, or by the very nature of their own "souls" or genetic predisposition, they may feel more inclined toward other members of their families, including the women. Some young men, by virtue of who they are, do not meet their father's expectations, or image of a "male." Some sons express parts of the father he has rejected, causing distance and struggle between them. However, nothing is set in stone; the formation of an identity complex is ongoing and impacted by many factors along the way.

Finding the Wild Man Within

Robert Bly has another view on the formation of male identity, based more upon the Jungian model.

"It can take a while for a son to overcome early negative views of the father," he says. "The psyche holds tenaciously to these early perceptions. Some mothers send out messages that what the father stands for is stiff, cold, and heartless. A man must confront these negative messages which have become deeply embedded within. When he gets in touch with his Wild Man (his true self) a real strength is added, the ability to live an authentic life. He's able to shout and say what he wants, to end that which is negative. This does not imply domination and treating others as though they were objects. In fact that kind of behavior comes about when the Wild Man cannot emerge. It becomes a substitute for the natural and primal force that men have cut themselves off from."

The struggle of many men is the integration of all parts of themselves, the need to be successful in the world, to conform to standards to achieve success and also to honor the wild one within. This task can seem so formidable that many do not even try to accomplish it. Jung discusses the crucial issue of integrating all aspects of ourselves. He says, "Nothing endangers the man's connection with his unconscious more than a successful life; it makes him forget his dependence upon his inner world."

The externally successful individual feels all his battles are outside of himself, and that it is through that type of success that he becomes a man. For Jung, this kind of struggle to be a hero represents an ambivalent struggle with the mother, who symbolizes the unconscious. To become a true hero the man must leave the primal union with the mother, or the unconscious, intuitive, feminine part of himself, and take charge of his destiny and perhaps the destiny of others as well.

When we look carefully at this model of male identity, we can then understand much about men, including their difficulty surrendering, in love, because this represents surrendering to the female once again.

Beyond issues with their mothers and fathers in the development of identity, many men get stuck, or fixated, at different points in time. If a trauma occurred at a certain age, or if there were developmental tasks which were incomplete, the individual sometimes can progress no further. As Søren Kierkegaard, the great philosopher said, "Spiritually, intellectually and psychologically, most men never grow past the age of fifteen."

Whichever point of view one subscribes to, the formation of identity is and must be an ongoing process. As a man grows, he meets new people and has different experiences, all of which change him and how he views the world. As a result of these encounters, he may reject certain role models he had once accepted, or he may discover new individuals who have qualities he wishes to adopt.

There are many parts in a person which clamor for attention and expression. At different points in his life, certain parts will come to the fore. Who we are, and can be, is ongoing and limitless. The good news is that identity is an evolving process; we all can and must evolve into newer and larger senses of ourselves.

Personal Inventory: Male Identity

The following categories are presented for greater understanding of the different parts of the male psyche. No one lives in just one category—each individual contains everything. Different parts of our psyche come forth at different points in our lives. As we go through each chapter, a full picture of each of these different types of men will develop.

Group A: Warriors, Heroes, Adventurers
Group B: Lovers, Dreamers, Peter Pans
Group C: Controllers, Perfectionists, Addicts
Group D: Wise Men, Gurus, Seers
Group E: A Real Guy!

SCORING
(Score each question from 1–4 in the following manner)

1. Not at all
2. Sometimes
3. Often
4. All the time

1. Does he speak often of the great or important men in his life?

2. Does he criticize himself and others frequently?

3. Does he love nature and spend time alone in it?

4. Does he constantly require a challenge? Is he tired or bored when nothing's going on?

5. Does he frequently search for the deeper meaning in events?

6. Is he always returning to someone or something that has happened in the past?

7. Does his interest wax and wane? Is he always seeking new stimulation?

8. Is he comfortable trying new activities, or going places he hasn't been before?

9. Does he demand you behave a certain way, and require a lot from you?

10. Is he preoccupied often, or lost in thought?

11. Does he handle surprises well?

12. Are his relationships long-term? Does he keep old friends?

13. Does he want more than life can give him?

14. Does he spend much time with his mother?

15. Does he plan special times together?

ANSWERS

Group A: Warriors, Heroes, Adventurers
(Questions 1, 4, 7) Score: 12 or more

If an individual scores 12 or more on the above questions he may well be in this category. This individual's basic identity includes a deep yearning to be larger than life, take on great challenges and accomplish large tasks. This should be factored into his life plan and encouraged.

Group B: Lovers, Dreamers, Peter Pans
(Questions 3, 14, 15) Score: 12 or more

These men require more intimacy than most. They greatly appreciate beauty and are hungry for romance. Some in this category have difficulty taking on adult responsibility and prefer a great deal of play.

Group C: Controllers, Perfectionists, Addicts
(Questions 2, 6, 9) Score 12 or more

These men focus upon controlling their external world, seeking to attain power over it. This often arises from a lack of a true sense of self-identity and control from within. They need to learn to let go and focus upon themselves.

Group D: Wise Men, Gurus, Seers
(Questions 5, 10, 13) Score 12 or more

These men have a deep need to understand the meaning of their lives, and seek a fuller experience of what living is.

Group E: A Real Guy
(Questions 8, 11, 12) Score 12 or more

These men are natural, real, able to live and let live. They have integrated or come to peace with the different parts of themselves.

The Hero

Jerzy, a sucessful, well-known artist, was born in a poor village in Europe and lived a life in which he constantly felt he had no idea how to belong.

"In my childhood, I suffered great inhibitions," said Jerzy. "I had a kind of shame that I was not the heroic person or prince I wanted to be, but just a lonely boy on the sidelines. A great shyness took over me as I had this inability to be the hero, or knight in shining armor, my mother wanted me to be. I loved her so much, but I felt I failed her because I could not be the kind of man she really admired.

"In kindergarten there were a lot of wild kids running around. I couldn't be a wild boy like them. I wanted to be a conqueror so my mother would be pleased. I felt she wanted a conqueror and that her love was conditional upon that. My father was a failure in the department of heroes, way below standard. He was meek and deferred to others and this caused her to constantly reject him. She let him and me know over and over that she admired a knightly person— a noble warrior. Of course I had no real idea how to be that."

In all men there is an unconscious archetype of the Hero, someone who can conquer all people and difficulties, who is invincible and never weak. Many men inherently believe this is the essence of a man, what women expect from them and what they expect from themselves as well. Unfortunately, many women join men in this fantasy, and project their own inner heroic qualities onto men.

In the past the job of the hero was specific—to slay dragons and giants, save the endangered woman, find hidden treasure, and protect the village or community. This can be called the role of the external hero, who had to face physical dangers. In our time, however, castles to storm and dragons to slay are in short supply. Organizations and bureaucracies have taken over the work of making the world safe. Standing up to these mammoth, impersonal organizations may be the most heroic external action a man can take today. However, the work of the internal hero is still open to all, regardless of his or her external circumstances. Anyone can take on the inner quest, which is the journey of becoming whole.

For many men, a hero is a mythical creature. Jerzy said he encountered heroes, ". . . Only in books. Though my cousin was a little like that. He was beautiful and wild and I was jealous of him, especially when I saw my mother noticing him and admiring his deeds. Because I was so preoccupied with all of this, I didn't know what might have been admirable about me, what my nature was. I was so driven to become a Hero, become number one—the great conqueror my mother wanted, if I couldn't be that, I decided I would be nothing. I had to be number one or nothing—so I became nothing much."

Jerzy's story is a remarkable example of how the false self develops, of how male identity is formed and supported by the fantasies and needs, not only of the unconscious, but of the dreams of the significant others in his family (or in reaction against them). If we listen closely to myths and fairy tales (which are read repeatedly to children), they teach a shocking lesson. Right from the start, children are taught to fulfill a larger-than-life image—to seek a role which will thrill others. This then gives the child a sense of significance, of having earned the right to be loved. He is taught he must earn his keep constantly. He is not taught that he is already perfect, already beautiful, complete and whole.

"One can never do or be enough to earn the love they are hungering for. Love is our birthright and must

> *come, simply because we exist, or it will not come at all."*
>
> —*Leonard Orr*

An idealized image presented to a young man that he cannot fulfill, is a source of frustration which can easily grow into rage. This self-hate is often turned against others. The need to be larger than life may well be related to the rash of teenage killings we are seeing today, where violence catapults the lonely, outcast teenager who feels he cannot fit the bill, into the role of a larger-than-life hero who is willing and able to act out smoldering feelings about himself and others, regardless of the consequences. The dragon these teenagers need to slay unfortunately becomes classmates or those they feel have abused them.

Self-Discovery

In order to discover and maintain who he truly is, a man must embark upon the crucial journey of self-discovery. He has to enter a deeper realm, go within, and not live solely according to external messages and injunctions. The man who undertakes this journey learns to listen to and honor his intuition, dreams, and feelings. He is taught to acknowledge and accept his own experiences, and knows there is a core within himself which will provide answers and direction. His entire life can then be an adventure of becoming more and more true to who he is.

Jerzy laughed as he recounted what a Hero means to him today.

"Finally, after many years, I have been able to outgrow my mother's images, to come to peace with the anger I held toward her for not loving me as I was. Now, to me, a Hero means one who has abandoned all these images and lives by what is true—lives by the real. In order to do that I had to finally tell her how I felt, and have her really listen. For years she could not listen to me. She brushed me off as weak, like my father. Naturally, I hated her for that. After I stopped hating her, and allowed my true self to arise more and more, no matter what she felt about it, finally one day, she was able to listen to what I said. I told her how I had always adopted a pattern, my whole life long, of trying to find out what the other person wanted me to be, and then trying to give them that. It never brought peace or satisfaction. In fact, in the long run there was anger with the person, for not knowing me as I was. After much struggle, one day I realized first I had to know and accept myself. It didn't matter how others felt about me. Only then did I become capable of love. Only then could my mother listen to me. And when she really did, she started to cry. I feel I only got through to her because I had first gotten through to myself."

Jerzy is a daring man who was brave enough to search the truth of his own life for himself.

William, a successful computer analyst in his forties, speaks about his sense of identity in a different way.

"It all came from my mother and grandmother," he said. "The first few years of my life my father was in the Navy and my mother and grandmother doted on me. The sun would rise and set with me; I was the center of their worlds. My grandmother constantly said, 'Billy is the best, the first, the smartest.' Years later, when other brothers came, she would say to them, 'Look at your brother, he's so smart, he's the best.' On the one hand I thought I was the best, on the other, what she said didn't make sense. After my father came home, he didn't react the same way to me. In fact, he started saying I was stupid. How could I be the smartest and stupid at the same time, I wondered. It didn't feel real. I knew I wasn't that smart, because there were things I didn't know. After all, I was still a kid. So, my identity became confused."

The Need to Be Perfect in Other's Eyes

When an individual is repeatedly told he is the best, smartest, kindest, this can also be experienced as a covert demand. He is expected to live up to another person's perception and his identity is imposed from the outside in.

"Another aspect of my sense of self," William continued, "was built upon them always telling me how handsome I was, how good I looked. I became constantly concerned with how I looked, wanting to see if that was so. I was also told, boys don't cry. 'How can a handsome boy cry like that? What do you want people to think? Smile. Don't you want people to think you're happy?' It was never, 'How do you feel?' It was definitely not okay to feel and express what was really going on. So I kept smiling. People would even say, I wish I could be like you, so happy and smiling all the time. But none of it was me."

William's entire sense of self was directed outwardly toward what other people thought of him and how he looked. When we try to find ourselves in the eyes of others, there is never anything stable to hold onto; people can change from day to day, and with them our sense of self. William always had to act a certain way, and there was no alignment between his external actions and inner experience. He couldn't know who he was, and neither could anyone else.

Sartre, the great French Existentialist philosopher and author, discusses this phenomenon in his biography of St. Genet. "We ascribe more reality to what others teach us than to what we learn by ourselves. Thus a man judges the appearance of what he is for others to be the reality, and the reality which he is to himself to be the appearance. A great confusion thus takes place."

How do we know we are of value? Through what we have accomplished? Through our feelings? Through our actions? Through the loving eyes of another, knowing what we mean to them? Knowing ourselves from the outside in requires wanting corroboration, affirmation, acknowledgment from others. Our entire lives may thus be spent looking in the mirror of another's eyes.

"This went on for years," said William. "I guess basically I was numb. I found a wife, married and had two children, and from the outside everything looked fine. Finally the game split apart when out of the blue my wife told me she was leaving. I couldn't understand what was going on. She said she felt she never knew me, was living with a stranger, and left.

"That was the first time I let myself cry. I cried like a baby for two days straight. Then I stopped crying and realized I was also a stranger to myself."

Toni Packer, teacher of meditation and awareness describes this condition beautifully. "What does it mean inwardly to want to be the best? It involves an idea of perfection. Trying to measure up to that image requires enormous ambition. That carries with it stressful side effects: strain, frustration, and maybe a growing callousness, or jealousy toward people who get in one's way. Striving to attain perfection cannot accomplish a relationship of kindliness and care with people around one. Rivalry and love do not exist side by side."

Living Behind a Mask

William lived behind a mask, with a persona, not a personality. This kind of disconnection from his real self contributed to the shell of a marriage, which finally cracked. His wife left, seeking more warmth and reality. That was the shock William needed and started him upon his search for who he really was.

"I spent lots of time walking at first, and then began taking workshops and classes emphasizing feelings and dreams. I went to places where there wasn't so much pressure to fit into a mold, and stopped trying to please everybody. Little by little I experimented with being who I was. It was scary at first, but worth it. For the first time, I began to have real fun."

Many men live lives encased in masks and armor they barely know is there. Driven by the need to fulfill roles they may not have ever chosen, they dread stopping to discover what is real. Stopping and making acquaintance with themselves, though, is crucial. When this happens, many symptoms of stress and addiction cease.

Everyone Who Lives Has Value

Sean, a young man in his late twenties, with a very successful twin brother, speaks of his sense of self as it relates to his brother.

"Since I was born," he said, "everyone always compared me to Robert. He was perfect. I was not. I was born a few minutes later and lived my whole life in his shadow. Whatever he did got applause. Whatever I did was forgotten. I lived a long time hating him, believing he took my life away. He had everything I wanted, especially my parent's love. Then, one day when we were seventeen, an amazing thing happened. Robert suddenly became very sick. From out of the blue, he was taken to the hospital late one afternoon. For a few days we didn't know if he was ever returning. Without him there, I realized that, by myself, I was whole. I wasn't him. I wasn't dying. Whoever I was, was completely fine, whether they liked it or not.

"Robert recovered and came home, but after that I was never the same. I didn't walk around in his shadow anymore. I didn't care how my parents viewed me. I realized we were all only here for a short time. Anyone could die any second. Everyone who lived was perfect and had a right to be there.

"People noticed the difference in me, but it didn't matter. They all asked me what happened. I didn't have an answer. I just felt good about myself. People sensed it, too, and started to pay more attention to me. I started getting invited to this and that, but people's views about me didn't matter to me anymore. I became my own best friend. Just the fact that I was here, breathing, seemed to be enough. Robert tried to get closer to me too. The whole thing was a huge surprise. Even though the whole family didn't want me to leave, after graduation I insisted upon going away to a college of my own.

"Once I was out of there I thought about what happened a lot. I realized that for my whole life I never felt whole, I never felt that I counted because I couldn't measure up to my twin. Now I don't measure myself up against anyone. Why measure yourself against someone who could be gone in a flash? I mean, what are we all anyway? What's so powerful or important about any of us? Who creates these measures, anyhow? Now I figure I'm fine just because God put me here. And so is everybody else. There's a huge freedom and happiness I now feel every single day. Now I choose the classes and work I want to do, and just do it. No matter what happens, each day I feel like I succeed."

Although he never called it that, Sean had an enlightenment experience, and discovered a sense of his fundamental value, and dignity, just because he was alive. His identity was no longer based upon measurement and comparison. He no longer had idealized images to live up to, was free to be himself and validate that. The close brush with the death of his twin brother woke him up to his true nature, and the true nature of life itself.

Interestingly enough, when Sean was able to acknowledge and validate himself, others around him began to do this as well. This is not surprising. The way others react to us often is a mirror of how we feel about ourselves. Rather than causing him to feel nihilistic, his experience of transience allowed Sean to be able to say yes to everything, and to be free to live with freedom.

Sean's interesting comment that he does the work he chooses and no matter what happens feels like he succeeds, points to his ability not to work for the praise of others, or to measure himself by external results. This is reminiscent of the philosophy of Morita, a Japanese psychiatrist who believes that all suffering and lack of self-worth is due to misdirected attention, and a wrong understanding of how character is built. In the Morita pathway, an individual is what he does, not what he imagines or thinks about. If he wishes to feel self-respect, he must undertake actions which are worthy of respect. He need not sit around waiting for some feeling of self-respect before he dares to act. An individual focuses upon his purpose in life and what is required of him; his sense of self never comes from the results of his actions, but simply from his undertaking the necessary acts. It is stressed that we can control our actions, but not their results. We do everything to the best of our ability, and are pleased with that. For Morita, identity and true sense of self arise from a life well-lived. Sean's present ability to live in this manner is a wonderful expression of this perspective.

Touchstones to Remember

1. Most men have only the vaguest idea of who they really are, or what is truly important to them. Much of a man's life is devoted to maintaining a fragile image of himself.

2. To look for oneself in the mirror of another's eyes brings sorrow and lack of stability. True identity is found within.

3. The identification with or rejection of the father plays a great role in the way a man sees himself.

4. Men need to find the "Wild Man" within, the part of themselves that is intrinsic to who they are and not

live life based solely upon social conditioning and external demands.

5. Some men become stuck or fixated at a certain age or point in development, especially if an unresolved trauma happened at that time. This has to be worked through so they can continue to grow.

6. Men who are close to their mothers may strive to become the kind of man she consciously or unconsciously longs for, in order to gain her love.

7. The False Self (or false sense of identity) is created by living according to the fears, dreams, and needs of others and the myths and demands of society. Living on this basis, we never find peace. We live an idealized image that is often based upon self-hate.

8. Unless we truly acknowledge and accept who we are at this moment, we can never grow into all we are meant to be.

THREE

Men, Power, and Control

The craving for power and control dictates the course of many men's lives. Some become obsessed with, and addicted to, power in its many forms. Their very sense of themselves as men is built upon how much power they feel they have, how much they can control the course of their lives, and the lives of others as well. While the need for power can have positive ends and be used constructively, unfortunately, in our society power is often confused with control. Power is seen as power to dominate and control something, not strength, stability, or a positive force. Power is defined as the power to build or tear down, not simply the ability to nurture, or the ability to love.

Personal Inventory: Men, Power and Control

Group A: Warriors, Heroes, Adventurers

Group B: Lovers, Dreamers, Peter Pans

Group C: Controllers, Perfectionists, Addicts

Group D: Wise Men, Gurus, Seers
Group E: A Real Guy!

SCORING
(Score each question from 1–4 in the following manner)

1. Not at all
2. Sometimes
3. Often
4. All the time

1. Is he flexible and relaxed when plans have to change?

2. Does he have friends and activities that are varied?

3. Is work his entire world?

4. Is he always seeking larger vistas? Can he be satisfied where he is for long?

5. Does he constantly ask his love partner about others they've known in the past?

6. Does he embark upon large projects that he finds thrilling?

7. Does he demand credit for most things and become depressed when he doesn't get it?

8. Does he do what he can in rough situations and then let it go?

9. Is he constantly worrying about the outcome of his work and efforts?

10. Does he fault himself and others relentlessly?

11. Is he able to focus himself deeply and remain silent and still?

12. Does he inspire and include others in his vision of life?

13. Can he surrender control to a higher power and be at peace?

14. Can he live a life that he respects?

15. Can he find fulfillment in love?

16. Does he use his power to help all people?

17. Does he use his power to enhance the quality of love in his life?

18. Does he make sure he's situated where he can be seen when out in public?

19. Can he delegate authority, share the power and control?

20. Can he completely give up the need to control others and the need to be controlled?

ANSWERS

Group A: Warriors, Heroes, Adventurers
(Questions 4, 6, 12, 19) Score 12 points or more

These men use power to conquer obstacles and achieve their visions and dreams. As they see life as a huge adventure, their need for control is not so great. Instead we find these individuals jousting with windmills, inspiring others, and living a life in which they can utilize all of themselves.

Group B: Lovers, Dreamers, Peter Pans
(Questions 5, 15, 17, 18) Score 12 points or more

These men convert their power into charm and magnetism, often used to attract a loved one, to be admired, and live a glamorous life. They spend considerable time trying to bring their fantasies to life, and enjoy both romance and all forms of the arts.

Group C: Controllers, Perfectionists, Addicts
(Questions 3, 7, 9, 10,) Score 12 points or more

These men hunger for both power and control. Often their strong need for dominance and authority masks the fact that they feel quite vulnerable basically and somewhat out of control. When this need intensifies it develops into various forms of addiction, which serve to numb the underlying anxiety they feel.

Group D: Wise Men, Gurus, Seers
(Questions 11, 13, 16, 20) Score 12 points or more

These men use their power to focus, be silent, be disciplined and control or dissolve inner and outer delusion and sorrow. Their power takes a quiet form, as they often live a life that is simple, harmonious and deeply in tune with all.

Group E: A Real Guy!
(Questions 1, 2, 8, 14) Score 12 points or more

These men use their power to live a natural, wholesome, outgoing life. They are often flexible during change and difficult situations, able to see a situation from all points of view, willing to compromise, and most of all, forgiving, both of themselves and others.

Addiction to Power.

When power is not channeled for the higher good, it can become the basis for addiction itself. It can be said that the road to recovery from addiction lies in the realization of where true power lies, how to use it constructively, and how to give up the false thrills unhealthy power supplies.

Joel Slavis, a very attractive single father in his forties, has been deeply engaged in working on his cravings for power and control. "I was going to college in the sixties," he said, "during the revolutionary period when everyone wanted to change the world. I was involved in the Vietnam War—all I wanted to do then was control and change the world."

Being involved in social and political action can be enormously exciting and create a sense of mission. While social and political activism has wonderful aspects to it, for many it can also be a way to escape personal issues that left unaddressed result in disaster.

The Need to Control

"I believe I have an addictive personality," Joel continued. "I've always wanted to control all kinds of things and could never understand why I couldn't. I always wanted people to behave the way I wanted them to. So, finally, this realization came to me that the solution to this is not to control. Instead of focussing upon others, I look at myself. I see myself as a person addicted to power and control. This takes my attention off the contest of wills, always being tugged and pulled. Living that way is very unpleasant. When I stop trying to control, I become more likeable, and others become more likeable too. I just look at people and think whatever they want to do is fine. I'm not God. It's a much easier way to get through. I can see addictive behavior in sex, in food. It's all a way of having power and control."

Joel considers himself a power addict who is now in recovery. "When you're craving power," he continued, "you can't think. You become very distorted. To want to control someone is basically an irrational thought that produces tunnel vision. So, if I can put the focus on myself rather than on trying to change everyone else, I'm a lot happier. Not controlling works in business too. Before, I was not really listening to the other person, just thinking how I could get the sale. I was not getting the information I needed about what the guy really wanted. When I'm not controlling, I'm able to really listen, and this works better for both of us."

By giving up his need to control others, Joel receives many wonderful returns. For the first time his mind is clear enough to be able to really hear others and know what they want. It also frees a great deal of energy for just enjoying his daily life.

"Not controlling also works to a degree with my caring for my daughter," Joel continued. "I keep reminding myself that she's her own person. It's been hard between us and she's getting older now. I have to step back to a certain extent. Otherwise I'm always forcing and pushing, and it doesn't work out anyway.

"When I just want to control everything I'm very unhappy. My body starts to crunch up and I can't sit back and relax. What I've started to do is to drink a glass of water, or keep a couple of glasses of water on my desk. That reminds me to come back to myself, take it a little easier."

Joel is using the water as an anchor, or tool, to create new associations in his mind. Whenever he drinks it, or sees it, he reminds himself to stop the old conditioning, take a deep breath, nourish himself, and remember who he really is, and what he wants in life. Addictive personalities usually love rituals, which provide a sense of structure and control. Channeling this need into the creation of constructive rituals reminds the individual to behave in a way that is for his, and other's highest good.

"My addictive behavior brought me to meditation," Joel continued, "to zazen. In meditation practice, you begin to realize that the world you think you're living in is smaller than the real world. You realize that there are other ways of looking at things. During meditation you learn how to take your attention off trying to control everything around you. This has now become a ritual with me. I go for a certain number of retreats a year. For it to be of any value you have to make a commitment. It's not meaningful to go once. You have to go over and over again."

In a sense Joel has replaced his addiction with a commitment to meditation. This is a wonderful step—replacing a negative habit with one that is positive. A true meditation practice will eventually free him from all compulsion, as he finds real security within himself.

Addiction to Money

"Western society is addicted to money," Joel says, "with getting it, spending it, hoarding it, it's all the same thing.

We're missing spirituality. Everything and everybody becomes a commodity. I just spent time with a very wealthy
man, who had hunched-over shoulders and was miserable.
Even though I work hard making money, I do not place ultimate value on it. I know what it's for now. It's an energy,
available to use. The question for me is how to use the energy in a positive way. My teacher, Eido Roshi, says when
you're reading a book you're not reading a book, it's reading you. It took me quite a while to understand that. Now I
realize what he means. So, I'm careful that money is not using me.

"There's a good book called *The Master's Game,* talking
about chasing money, power, spirituality. The more you
chase it, the further it goes. But the value of money is to
take care of things. If not used wisely, it makes lots of people
unhappy. A lot of people have the illusion that it's their security, but even if they have money, other forms of insecurity, illness, and loss still can happen. Money can't protect
you from that.

"I'm in better shape now than when I was twenty," Joel
continued. "Now I'm starting to really grow up, take responsibility, realize what life is for. When you're not addicted to substances, including money, sex, and power, you
get closer to your higher consciousness, which is a true
high—your real spirituality."

In recognizing his addiction to power and control Joel took
the first step in breaking free, and being able to experience
growth in many areas of his life. The need to control and the
hunger for power is so basic to most men, and so reinforced
by the society, that it is difficult to view this as an addiction,
as toxic as any substance. The experience of power over another, and the feeling of high it can bring, is a replacement

for strong sense of self and personal direction. It comes out of weakness, not strength, and masks the fear and emptiness that lay behind it. It is therefore crucial for men to see the consequences, both upon themselves and those they care for, of living as a power addict.

Addiction to Others' Expectations

Dr. Winn Henderson, a well-known radio personality, who hosts the internationally syndicated show, *Share Your Mission*, author, and founder and director of a clinic devoted to recovery, was once, too, in the grip of addiction.

"I probably got started just like everyone else," said Dr. Henderson. "When I grew up, I was expected to achieve and perform extremely well in school. I was considered intelligent, expected to go to college and do something important. So, I got into a habit of doing things without thinking about what the total picture was. I became a medical doctor and started seeing patients. Most of us just follow along, go to school, make the grade, graduate from college, get married, go into a profession. Most people do that without any deep searching for the meaning of life. Until you get to the point where it gets really important to you to search out answers to spiritual questions, it's easier and more comfortable to go along with what's happening at the time and not spend any significant amount of time thinking. I believe that's what most people do, until they have a problem. Then they have to take time to really stop and think about it."

One could say that behaving in this manner produces a feeling of power, the power of belonging to the group and receiving its support and approbation. This gives rise to a sense of control and security in one's life, as though one has the entire society behind him and the comfort of group respect.

This is addiction to belonging to the group, being afraid to be different or to think for oneself. There is a fear of non-conformity and the dangers it could hold. However, many great psychologists, including Jung and Adler, tell us that it is crucial to an individual's growth and mental health that he develop the ability to *individuate*, to step out from the group or family unit, to be one's own self.

> "I had a wife, a daughter, a practice," Dr. Henderson continued, "and then my wife and I got divorced. She took my daughter and moved halfway across the country. I was alone. The break-up of one's family is one of the more stressful experiences in a person's life. So, at that time, I fell apart a little bit. I was single and had a lot of money, and you know how that might be."

At a time of radical change or despair it's easy to grab for anything that makes us feel good on a short-term basis. This search for quick peace of mind, or gratification, is the basis of many addictions. It comes from the feeling of being out of control, and not having the power to face the situation and one's feelings head on.

> "I tried to make up for the emotional hurt," Dr. Henderson continued, "and my lack of understanding of the deeper significance of where I was in life, and what I needed to be doing about it, got me into this whole spiral. I started producing more, seeing more patients, making more money, working longer hours. I worked from seven in the morning until two in the morning. It started taking a toll."

Addiction to Work

Dr. Henderson has described workaholicism taken to the extreme. The anguish which Dr. Henderson could not face directly, fuelled him to work in an addictive and compulsive way. The long hours of work and many patients produced a false sense of power and sense of mastering his destiny.

"I truly believe," Dr. Henderson continued, "that had I continued that way, with all the things that were going on, with all the people that were attached to me, and drawing from me, emotionally and financially, that I probably would have died. It was too much, but I couldn't stop it."

When we grab at something to give us false power, eventually and inevitably what we grab at gains power over us. It controls our lives and we become unable to live without it.

"I wanted to retire and get out of the spiral," Dr. Henderson continued, "and do something else. I knew something was missing. I couldn't be happy in life just making money and running. But at that time I didn't know what the answer to this was. Right around then, a difficult scenario developed. Things spiraled out of control. I got a retirement, but not on my terms. In that respect, I really got what I was asking for, but in a way I never imagined. What happened next was almost as bad as having my family ripped away from me.

"I was working as many as nineteen hours a day, many hours of which I was seeing poor patients on a free basis and often taking on patients other doctors refused to treat. In this surreal atmosphere, my compulsive behavior of trying to help everyone reached its zenith.

"I was interested in addiction medicine, and realizing that

a substantial number of patients I was seeing suffered from nervousness (anxiety), I began a clinical study on the long-term value of Valium (the world's most prescribed anti-anxiety drug at the time).

"Although completely legal, my study increased the number of prescriptions I wrote for Valium well above the number written by other physicians in my area. This in turn came to the attention of federal investigators who were looking into drug distribution patterns in the government's 'War on Drugs.' Federal investigators, frustrated by not being able to find evidence of over-prescribing over a long period of time, entered into a conspiracy with one of my employees to get an indictment for attempted bribery of a federal official. I was in a "no win" situation, but because of my arrogance, I went to court expecting to be exonerated.

"Next thing I knew I was in a federal holding cell without any light, except for one hour a day. I was able to get the bed closest to the door, so the light was a little better. Then it got worse. All kinds of things started happening. I considered myself a prisoner of war in that particular situation—the government was warring on drugs and taking its own citizens as prisoners.

"So, I was really confused because I thought this should not have happened to me. I didn't understand why it happened. I felt it was not fair that it happened. I kept wondering what's going on here? I started praying for an answer."

When pushed to the extreme, some turn in a direction they would have never taken. In Dr. Henderson's case, he turned to prayer. This move on his part, opened up a whole new world for him.

"One night I had this dream," he continued, "and it was very, very real. In it I was told that the reason this had happened, the reason I was here, was that there was some information that needed to be brought out to the world, and I was the one to do it. That information turned into my first book which was called, *The Cure of Addiction*. In this dream I was told to write the book, and that as soon as the book was done, I'd be freed.

"So, the next morning I got up and got a pad of legal paper, and according to the outline I was given in the dream, wrote the book. People helped me along the way. There was a counselor who helped me with a number of little things, like getting pencils and paper and getting me out a number of hours in the day to be able to see. I was moved from here to there, all over the place in the next two years. Things improved quite a bit later on. There were good times and bad times. You can imagine how difficult it would be with nobody in charge wanting you to do anything productive. In fact, when they knew about it, they would do whatever they could to keep me from accomplishing my mission. So, it took a little time to get the book out. But, finally, two years later, the book was published, and within forty hours of my receiving the first copy, I was freed. I told people the whole two years that I would get out when it was done. They said, 'You're crazy,' and so forth. That book got me launched on my new work. That was how it started, I knew I had a mission to accomplish, a purpose for the rest of my life."

A Man with a Mission

In a sense, Dr. Henderson's experience can be read as a metaphor for all of our lives. There are many kind of jails people live in: psychological jails, where they are tortured by thoughts, images, memories, and feelings; and the jail of cravings and addictions. These kinds of jails can often be worse than the physical pain of being locked up. However, once we know and undertake our mission, we become free. Freedom is gained by the positive use of power, channeling the forces of our will to accomplishing something positive for all.

"At that point," Dr. Henderson continued, "I dedicated what was left of my life to pursuing my mission. Part of it is to help people recover from addictions. There's not one person who I've ever interviewed, who has not come to grips with the four questions in my book, that is not addicted to something or other. Even when I go into churches, and talk to devoutly religious people, I find many have an addiction to negative thinking. They see the negative, bad side of life, or are co-dependent and have control issues, trying to control other people and family. To me one addiction is no better or worse than any other. It doesn't matter if you have a problem with the bottle, or with drugs, relationships, it's all the same, because the problem comes from an empty feeling, a hollow feeling inside of not knowing the four questions, the answers to them, and being able to apply them to one's life.

"These four questions that we must all think of and answer are: *Who am I? Where do I come from? What am I doing here? Where am I going when I'm done?*"

These questions are the essence of all religious and spiritual practice. "Truth is truth regardless of how you get it. I come from a Christian perspective, so this is how I answer them. Who am I? A child of God. Where did I come from? I came from God. What am I doing here? I'm doing God's will. Where am I going when I'm done? I'm returning to God. The difficult part is applying it. I teach people how to apply it."

Lack of Self-Esteem

"For example, most of the problems that we confront in life, especially psychological and physical illness, come from a lack of self-esteem, a feeling that we're not important, not good enough. However, living the answers to these questions, knowing we are children of God, we realize that we need to take care of ourselves and should not do things to ourselves that are harmful. People try to improve their self-esteem in the short run by looking around in the environment trying to figure out what makes them feel good. For some it might be alcohol, drugs, other people, food, control, drugs, whatever. Short-term it improves your self-esteem and makes you feel good. But, long-term it doesn't, because every addictive behavior has side effects, and most of them are bad. Often you don't understand it when bad things happen.

"The only way to break addiction is through understanding what true relationships are, especially if you realize and understand that you are a special creation, created by God. If you don't know it or believe it, you have problems because you think you're not valuable or are dispensable."

Dr. Henderson lives the answers to his questions. His life is a testimony to a man who has not only found the cure to addiction, but has created a deeply meaningful, fulfilling life, not only for himself, but for all he touches.

The Power of the Organization

Another man with a mission is Lt. General Anthony Lukeman, newly retired from the U. S. Marines. He has lived his whole life dealing with power, and in his eyes, the power of the organization is positive—it can be used to build character and purpose, especially when it is directed toward ends that are based upon the highest ethics and integrity. Rather than being addicted to power, Lt. General Lukeman sees power as a tool which he and others used to grow.

"What I really believe in has come from my time in the Marine Corps," he said, "from being in that kind of organization, which gave me a true understanding of responsibility."

Strength and Character Are Innate in People

Lt. Lukeman believes ethics are a large part of the value of his time in the Marines.

"Real power is ethical conduct. As I see power and men, power must be used to do what's right and become all you can be. I've spent a great deal of time helping young people in the Marines to grow. Maybe a place to start is with the realization that the talent in people is already there. You don't put character or strength into people, what you do is bring out the strength and character that's already there. That's an old thought, but it's a very significant part of the way I think. You've got young people who come from all kinds of places, in many cases from strong families, in other cases terrible families, or no family. They are all reaching toward something, or not reaching toward something because they've never been lead to it. I've had wonderful experiences in dealing with all these young people, found it very inspiring."

For Lt. General Lukeman all the power and control at his disposal was channeled toward the highest good both for the individuals, the organization and the nation as a whole.

"The reason I've loved working with the Marines is that decisions are not based upon economic motives," he continued. "In the private sector I think a lot of them are. In business, it doesn't make any difference what you're talking about, the bottom line is money. A second and very obvious reason that ethics are involved here in the Marines are the human stakes. They are, at times, as high as they can be. The decision to attack, or defend, or use supporting arms, to understand the terrain, any of those kinds of decisions, they're going to present the risk of some people getting killed. As a result of this Marines have very little choice when it comes to following orders."

For some the imperative to follow orders in such a unilateral way can be seen as a loss of freedom, the ultimate expression of another's control. However, this kind of surrender to the highest good can also give freedom of another kind— the freedom to act without hesitation, without having to stop and consider all of one's options continually.

"There is power in following, and also it has dangers. What we want is to have those young people stand up and say, 'General, that's not a good way to proceed, this is the way we should do it.' We want them to come forth directly in the right way, not through covert means. But if you tell them to do something, they have to. They must be trained this way because their life or others' lives may be at stake."

In our society, surrender of personal wishes to the highest good is a value that is practically extinct. This is related to the loss of the Hero, (who sacrifices himself for a greater cause) and the absence of role models who command sufficient respect for young people to trust and follow them. In place of this we find a ridiculing of authority and general cynicism culminating in random violence, even in the schools.

Unless this is mended, the entire fabric of man's well-being has no place to stand.

True Authority Is Power

"So you have to use whatever authority you have very judiciously. True authority is power and when used wisely it is a great advantage. Remember also that the political, military stakes are very high. We use a euphemism, and say national defense. It's important to the defense of the individual liberty of this great democracy that we have leaders who think like this, who are able to subjugate their own personal responses to the greatest good for all concerned.

"Another reason authority is crucial here is this absolute need to win. This translates into a lot of other things—there must be absolute trust, and common dedication to the mission and responsibility of looking out for other humans involved. In the civilian aspects of our lives it really translates into this too. There's a higher regard for truth and objectivity in the Marine Corps than any other organization I've been in. It has to do with training and the quality of the individual, and the stakes, their ability to learn and ability to lead. It was a big surprise to me as I started dealing more with civilians and other services that this focus upon absolute truth and honesty is indeed unique to the Marines. It's great to have it. There is also an incredible level of support from a group when they live within this code of conduct."

Channeling Aggression and Violence

The Marines may be a way to channel the aggressive or violent nature of some men. Lt. General Lukeman said, "First of all, war is probably inevitable and going to involve killing.

But aggression and violence can be positive if used toward positive ends, such as killing to protect others and make the world safe."

Although one might disagree with the view that killing can ever stop killing, what we are witnessing here is aggression in men, disciplined, channeled, and used to serve principles that one believes are for the good of the country. Of course, a thorough examination of how this aggression is used is imperative, if one is not going to get caught in justifying violence in the name of the highest good.

Translating these Principles into Civilian Life

Lt. General Lukeman feels that these principles can be applied to the problems with youth at risk we have today. He said,

"Accept responsibility, be able to delegate authority, and carry this further than most people would consider legitimate. I mean *love responsibility*. Then when you pass the authority onto others, you have to know and trust that they can do what has to be done. The last thing you want to do is stand over them. What I wonder about is, who is taking this kind of responsibility in the school systems today? We have huge problems in the school systems, because responsibility doesn't exist and family doesn't exist, so if we talk about family values, since it doesn't exist, many students are not going to get that from the family. I honestly think that the institution we call the schools will have to pick up the responsibility as we go on. We truly need some leaders willing to do that, and to stand up and out for good values and the teaching of them.

"Another way we can use a principle of the Marines in

the school system is *Take Action and Don't Whine. Never Whine!* Get the job done. Remember, the mission isn't more important than the people, or the people, they're coequal.

"Planning is another crucial step. *Plan to the best of your ability, but then when it comes to putting it in action, remember, it's not going to be exactly what you planned*. Then you've got to be right on the spot, making sure action happens despite the changes. *Be positive. You've got to be positive. If you can't you'll never succeed.*

"What are the risks? *Know what could keep you from achieving your goals*—complacency, indifference (feeling there's not much I can do) and the opposite—excessive self-confidence. Lowering your standards is also a great danger. *Don't lower standards*. People always want to lower standards for the best reasons. In the military some years ago there was a project called project one hundred thousand. This was an attempt to go after young people who were not basically high school graduates, with an ability to score well on tests, individuals who would not have been included in the past. Many of them would be going on to Vietnam, and the idea was that this would be good for the country, and for the military services; that both the military and the young people would benefit. But, because we lowered the standards so much, it didn't work. It was a failure. We had nothing but trouble and upsets from this. A result was that you had a lot more problems than successes. There was a very good national and social reasons that said don't worry about the national tests, don't worry about high school graduation, even though we know that if they don't do well in those areas, they're not going to stay in. Not lowering standards is an especially important directive to apply to the schools today.

"These are the issues we are faced with now in the society. They are confusing and I think it contributes to the violence we are seeing in the young people everywhere because there are no uniform standards, no clear cut roles, everything is shifting and up for grabs and this creates tremendous insecurity in kids and the sense that the world is crumbling around them. A lot of it has to do with a Right Now attitude. The thing that's important is right now. At some point, I would hope, in a young person's life, he is already thinking of the future, how to get somewhere close to his God-given talents and pass it on to the next generation. In my view this is what real power entails."

This is an intense statement in support of the need for power and control informed by higher values and a large vision. When power and control are transformed into discipline and structure, this strengthens individuals and allows them to harness and utilize their full capacities. It also builds character, the ability to delay personal gratification, and to think of others before oneself. Particularly now, when traditional structures are being discarded, the need for discipline and values cannot be overemphasized.

Touchstones to Remember

1. When the need for power and control are not channeled for the highest good, they can become the basis of addiction itself. All addiction produces a false high, and ultimately places one more out of control.

2. By giving up the need to control others, there are many wonderful returns.

3. Be careful about money—make sure it is not using you. Discover where your real security lies.

4. The questions that reveal an individual's mission in life are: *Who am I? Where do I come from? What am I doing here? Where am I going?*

5. The need for false power and control come from a lack of self-worth and self-esteem.

6. Strength and character exist in everyone, they only need to be brought out.

7. The ability to follow, and surrender to the highest good can bring the greatest freedom of all.

8. True authority is power—authority used for the good of all.

9. To attain true authority, love responsibility, delegate authority, take action and don't whine. Be positive. Know what could be keeping you from achieving your goals.

FOUR

Men and Work

Many men identify themselves through the work they do, their level of success and position they've gained in the hierarchy. In this manner they are responding to a deep hunger to take on large tasks and challenges, accomplish them successfully, and be rewarded in the community by their peers. These needs are primal and hark back to the days when man was a warrior, hunting for food, providing for his family, and fighting wild animals and other enemies.

When there are not external enemies to take on, or large tasks to accomplish, internal enemies raise their heads, illusory insults, losses and fears obsess the mind, and men fight randomly, without purpose. Road rage grows, wives are beaten, gangs erupt into violence. In the case of true physical danger, such as during war, these disparate elements in man's psyche become focused, and are mobilized against an acceptable external cause.

For many men, work is war. They are there to slay dragons, prove their prowess and their ability to keep themselves and their families alive. Some men become "external" warriors, focusing on conquests in the outside world; others become "internal" warriors, slaying demons that attack from within. These internal warriors would agree with the quote by Taisen Desimaru, Zen Master and Martial Arts Expert: "Any conflict, whether it takes place within the body and mind, or outside them, is always a battle against the Self."

Personal Inventory: Men and Work

Group A: Warriors, Heroes, Adventurers
Group B: Lovers, Dreamers, Peter Pans
Group C: Controllers, Perfectionists, Addicts
Group D: Wise Men, Gurus, Seers
Group E: A Real Guy!

SCORING
(Score each question from 1–4 in the following manner):

1. Not at all
2. Sometimes
3. Often
4. All the time

1. Does work consume most of his thoughts in and out of the office?

2. How good is his relationship with his boss?

3. How good is his relationship with peers and clients?

4. How many "meaningful" challenges must he face every day?

5. If he never came into the office again, how good would he feel?

6. How often does he dream of doing other work?

7. How important is the money he makes, or other rewards?

8. How important is the status provided?

9. How open and honest can he be every day?

10. If he could do anything at all he wanted, how likely is it he would be doing the job he is doing? How much does he dream of doing creative work?

11. Is he stable and balanced regardless of the outcomes he faces every day?

12. Does he feel he serves all of humanity in the work he does?

13. How much is his work a means of attaining more and more power?

14. How high are the stakes he is facing? How close to being life and death?

15. How much danger must he face in the work he does?

16. How much does he need to have authority over others?

17. How much of himself does he share with others at work?

18. How meaningful does he find his work in the larger picture?

19. How close is the work he is doing to his ultimate dream?

20. How much does this work provide glamour and charisma?

ANSWERS

Group A: Warriors, Heroes, Adventurers
(Questions 4, 7, 14, 15) 12 points or more

These men require challenge and adventure to make their work worthwhile. They thrive upon overcoming huge obstacles and living with stakes that are high. Some even have to face real danger every day. Unless these factors are present, no matter what they do, they will not feel as though they are using all parts of themselves or are fully alive.

Group B: Lovers, Dreamers, Peter Pans
(Questions 5, 9, 10, 20) 12 points or more

For these men the workplace is not the main arena where they find satisfaction or sense of self-worth, unless it happens to include creativity, and is then not perceived as work. For these men relationships are most crucial, and especially their ability to see themselves as free spirits, with the ability to be open and loved.

Group C: Controllers, Perfectionists, Addicts
(Questions 1, 8, 13, 16) 12 points or more

For these men work is a main arena where they can garner power and control. This is the test of their self-worth, and usually these men thrive most when they have authority over others and receive constant affirmation that they are in control. These men can easily become workaholics, using the power attained at the workplace to block out other needs and demand the same respect everywhere else. In this case work becomes a drug and the person can require higher and higher doses.

Group D: Wise Men, Gurus, Seers
(Questions 12, 17, 18, 19) 12 points or more

For these men work becomes a way of expressing their highest vision, and serving humanity. They strive for the highest values, and often teach, write, speak and communicate their deep feelings about what life is all about. These men do not view work as work, but as a mission or calling which their lives are dedicated to.

Group E: A Real Guy!
(Questions 2, 3, 6, 11)

These men receive satisfaction and enjoyment both from the work itself and the daily interaction with other individuals there. Personal relationships, openness and sharing are important to them, as well as the quality of the work they do. They are usually able to remain balanced, no matter what results come, and return to the simple pleasure of what they do.

The External Warrior

Ed Pankau, nationally known private detective, speaks about men's need for adventure and challenge, of the external warrior each man craves to be.

"I think that lots of men really live for a challenge," he said. "It's part of that biological imperative—basically we are hunters, and men like to hunt, whether it's a relationship, a client, or a deal. Some find fulfillment in marriage, but many don't. In my business I see people who have no challenge left in their life and there's nothing they feel they live for, so they create trouble, and then I have to hunt them down.

"Men need a mountain to climb. When people retire, the life goes out of lots of them. The more active a person's life has been, the more danger. All policemen are hunters. When the challenge goes away, then they lose their will and reason to live. To a lesser extent, marriages are the very same thing. A guy's got to have a challenge, a reason to get up and fight the battle every day."

Mr. Pankau perceives challenges as battles or fights, and also as the ability to express one's individuality. He said,

"Corporate America presents enough challenge for some, maybe, but when it's all group decisions it gets too bland. There's very little room for individuality left. To me, individuality is the most important thing. To be able to do something yourself. That's the original American dream—individual enterprise and getting out there to be able to express yourself. Being able to do that is a high, believe me."

Constantly living with obstacles and challenge can keep a man "high" or in a state of continuous excitement, feeling as though he is climbing mountains, proving his prowess day by day. But what about when challenges subside, or the mountain becomes too high? How does a man like this deal with the challenge of inner losses, with changes and life transitions that necessarily affect all lives? Many men are lost at times like these. They have not developed qualities that would prepare them to deal with it. It may be easier for them to climb high mountains than to face inner feelings, or intimacy between them and their partners.

The need to continually conquer challenges can also keep these obstacles and problems present in their lives. Some men are not comfortable without some problem to solve, so if they don't have one at hand, they create it quickly. Completion, rest or fulfillment can never then take place.

For Ed Pankau and others who perpetually overcome challenges, this kind of lifestyle can combat the feeling of being numb, weak, of not finding meaning or satisfaction in life as it is. Pankau said,

> "Men have got to be firing on all cylinders. There are other ways than work to achieve it, but in our culture, for men, most of their excitement, adventure and challenge comes through work. It wakes the whole person up and allows him to use all of himself. And work is the only place many men can experience that. Some try to get it in their relationships with women, but once you have her it loses something, the challenge is gone."

Ed Pankau is an example of an external warrior who must constantly be conquering windmills, winning battles, escalating the push in his life. There is much productivity and creativity which is of value in this lifestyle, but years of living at this intensity can drain him physically and emotionally. A man like this may find himself unable to be comfortable and secure at home, alone by himself. Without his work and conquests to define him, he may feel useless, and thus prone to depression and despair.

Money and Work

Pete, a vice president in charge of sales and marketing of a computer firm, is another example of an external warrior, someone who has dedicated his work life to external success—in his case, represented by money and the goods it can provide.

> "I'm married with three children—two girls and a boy. I'm fairly successful, but lately my work hasn't been so satisfying. It's not so challenging anymore. It's too easy. I do better when I'm challenged and pushed. If I'm not pushed I become kind of lazy. What I'd like to tell you about my work is that sometimes I take money, maybe a thousand dollars or so, for expenses that aren't real. This perks things up for me. Makes me feel it's all worth it.
>
> "I'm partially in control of the books and am able to put in expenses that aren't real. I enjoy doing it because I feel like getting away with it. In a certain sense it's mine—I've earned it. I don't take as much as the other partners, but I do it and just buy stuff, go out to eat, get some clothes. Mostly it disappears. I disappear money. I remember my father used to say, the way you spend money you'll never have any. I don't know if it's a curse or something, but boom—even if I try to save, it doesn't happen. I always said my father's not right about me, but then he turns out to be right after all. I don't want to do this necessarily, but I feel like I can't help it. I'm in a kind of double bind."

Because the work he is doing is essentially unfulfilling to him—and all his rewards are external—Pete must even find ways of keeping himself rewarded that are against his sense of personal honesty and integrity. He is working for what he can "get"—not for pleasure or pride in the work itself, but for the cash it brings.

He is also responding to messages from his childhood. Even if we resist our parents, and do not want to take in what they've said about us, many find themselves living out their parents' words. The child lives on within us and despite difficulties we may have had with our parents, deep down we still want to honor them, believe they are right, and gain their approval. By his behavior now, Pete is making what his parents said about him in childhood true.

"Not only do I take that extra money," said Pete, "but I could take three thousand, and in ten days I don't have a dime. I have nothing to show for it. Even though I have a good job, underneath it, I am disappearing the family's savings."

This kind of behavior also represents rage in Pete, the desire to sabotage himself and his efforts, not to allow himself to have the rewards he obtains. It is a covert way of expressing his enormous dissatisfaction not only with his work but with his entire lifestyle.

> "I spend money we don't have. I think my wife must know. She handles the bills and says the way you spend we'll never have any money. I demand a large allowance though. It's a business account. I take people out to lunch, travel, taxis, etc. I sit in a cab and watch the meter and want it to get higher. I feel like a money drunk. I can't wait to give away more money. We have a big debt, considering that we should have a good savings. I thought about seeking help with this, but never did. I don't have a savings account. I'm making six figures and I save nothing."

Pete is not unlike many men who both crave and discard the money they make. Symbolically speaking, this is an example of actually working for nothing. It is a way of saying that who he is and what he does has no intrinsic value. All he wants is a form of instant gratification, to get his needs met on the spot. "If I get ahead, or a bonus or something, it's gone before it comes. Even paychecks. So, it's like I work for nothing."

Pete does not experience joy in his work, or pleasure in providing for his family. He said,

> "I work for the government, for taxes. I have obligations, so I have to work. Sometimes I don't really know why I'm working. Not any more. Still, I do what I have to and don't complain. But what do I get from my wife? Complaints. Always about money. Why are you buying this? What are these toys? We have one of these, why do we need another one?"

His behavior with money is naturally affecting his marriage. Although on the surface Pete works hard, his resentment and sense of meaninglessness spills over to his wife, and he refuses to provide appropriately. On the one hand he gives, on the other he takes away—by not providing savings and by accumulating debt. Not only is he sabotaging himself, but also his wife and family.

Pete said, "I like to spend, to shop and look around. Actually I realize that money has become a God for me, a source of life, reprieve and happiness. And deep down I know it's nuts. How can I step off this treadmill?"

Pete doesn't think it is possible to step off the treadmill. "Can you?" Pete asked, surprised. "Can anyone? Except into the ground? Then you're off it, when you're six feet under. I don't know what happens then."

Bill Solomon, a teacher of the Avatar method for self-development, commenting on this says,

> "The only time you get off that treadmill is when you realize that you are the source of your life experiences, and take

responsibility for what's happening to you. Pete has to stop and take a long, hard look at his values about work and money. He must also understand what his beliefs are. When you do this, you then can discard those values and beliefs that are not suitable and choose those that feel right to you. Then external events won't be compulsively driving you.

"If Pete handled his beliefs about money, that would be a very helpful thing. He should ask himself, "What do I believe about money? How does this connect with my beliefs about life and relationships? His father's comment to him that the way he spends money, he'll never have any, is a belief. This belief then creates the experience, and it all looks true. What Pete must realize is that the belief comes first. If he changes his beliefs, he'll change his experiences. Let him ask himself what kind of experience he'd like to create, then write down a list of beliefs he'd need to create that. Next step is to take the positive beliefs on. He'll see his life turn around."

Pete, however, has no connection with his inner life, and has made money and goods the essence of his focus. The emptiness and futility he is expressing are an inevitable outcome of that. In order to escape the trap that Pete is in, a man needs to focus upon both his inner and outer worlds. He must work both to meet financial needs and also to express his values, and make a contribution to others. He must feel his work makes a difference, and serves a larger good. When work does not include self-expression and the fulfillment of a vision, sooner or later it backfires, and no matter how much money has been acquired, a feeling of emptiness sets in.

The Interior Warrior

Alan, an architect in Vermont, in his early thirties, is sensitive, enterprising and successfully runs his own business.

The challenges Alan faces on the work front are inner, emotional, and about how he is as a human being. Along with the tangible challenge of his daily tasks, the quality of his personal relationships are very important to him.

"One thing that bothers me terribly about work," Alan said, "is that if you have somebody who works for you, or a client, and you're nice to them, it seems the nicer you are and the more obliging, the more they want. Instead of reciprocating the kindness, they think you are a pushover, and become more demanding, and unpleasant to work with. To my great distress, I have found this with many of my clients. The clients, however, where I'm not as nice—where I'm curt or rushed or don't give them as much attention—almost always are much nicer to me. In fact, one client I was not nice to and I felt bad about it, and the very next day she FedExed me flowers."

Alan feels he has to modify his behavior because of these tendencies in others.

"I have to check myself before being too nice to somebody, I have to be careful of what I'm saying, become slightly cold and set very professional boundaries. Otherwise I realize I'm setting myself up for trouble. I think relationships get set up instantaneously. If you oblige them by returning their calls twelve times a day, the calls increase. Whereas, if you lay off, and don't return their call for a week, they develop that expectation and don't take it for granted that you'll be there whenever they want you. If you indulge people it becomes set in stone very quickly and it's hard to break it."

The False Self

Alan is struggling with the false persona he needs to assume on the job and the ways in which it encases him and separates him from what is satisfying. He says,

"I'm forced to behave in a way I don't like. And then before I know it, I become that person. That's hard. I think to a certain extent that's how businessmen become who they are—cold, curt and often unfeeling. It's because on a deeper level people will treat you the way you let them. They will take from you what you allow them to take. Unfortunately, most people are more into taking then giving. Work can be a source of combat."

Alan values other aspects of life, which the nature of business itself seems to shut out for him. He is an eloquent spokesman for the way many men feel, but may not be aware of, or verbalize, even to themselves. Alan speaks to the need to bring vitality and deeper human connection into the workplace.

"Business makes you lonely," Alan continued, "because you have to be detached. You can't have the kind of closeness and warmth you want in your day, because if you become friendly, others become suspicious of your skills. I had a client once and I visited him far away and I decided that weekend I would just drop the whole professional front and be warm and friendly. It was a disaster. We just casually hung out as if we were friends. Then sure enough, when I called him a few weeks later, he never returned the call— and then he ended up not being my client anymore.

"I've noticed this several times. If you don't maintain a professional front they doubt your professionalism. If you become warm and friendly, it's upsetting. I think there are lots of people who would like to give warmth and kindness, but when you start giving it to them, they become suspicious, or can't allow themselves to have it, and so they start thinking that something is wrong with you.

"I've seen this with women, too. I've seen women who are extremely nice, warm and open with clients and they persistently have a hard time getting the clients. But when they develop a curt, hard edge to them, they do better. Clients somehow see authenticity in that curtness. That means they're good.

"I think that men live a lonely existence at work. You often see, for instance, a rough, aggressive telemarketer, or stockbroker or car salesmen, a whole breed of men who you see acting this way. I'm sure most of these men weren't like that until they got into their profession. They go into this world and learn that if you make a call and want to keep the person's interest, you're not nice and sweet, but tough. Then, after you make several thousand calls like that and start hearing yourself a thousand times, you brainwash yourself and become that pattern. That happens to other professions as well.

"Both men and women who stay in business on a corporate level become cold and hard because that's what they've learned how they survive in a corporate environment. I've had women tell me all the time they've learned to become a bitch in the environment so they'll succeed. As I see it, this is too high a price to pay. That's how it has to be if you want to maintain the relationship. There are a few real relationships, but very few."

The concern of the "internal warrior" is always with "real relationships" both with others and with himself. Despite all his or her conquests in the external world, they feel ultimately empty if the human connection has not been made.

Fortunately for Alan, his false self doesn't spill over into his other relationships. "My friends are my friends and they take me as I am or not at all. With my friends, I lay it on the line right away. That's how I like to be with people in general. But you can't be that way with your clients, so you feel like you're living this false life."

The sense of being false at work, constantly playing a role, ultimately takes its toll on the individual. It robs much of the pleasure and nourishment that can be had through interpersonal contacts, and distances him from how he is feeling, and what truly matters to him. Over time this contributes to the experience of "burn-out," the sense of being unable to go on any longer, that there is nothing to draw upon inside. An individual can only play a role for so long without losing contact with who he is, his natural resources, and that which makes life and work a joy for him.

Work and Identity

Alan suggests there may be an antidote.

"The person who's working in that environment should constantly remind himself that his true identity is not who he has to be at work. If he's aware he's playing a role, perhaps he can live with it, as long as he knows he's not that role. Otherwise, twenty or thirty years go by and he turns around and has become a stranger to himself. Then, if he's fired or laid off and goes into another role, he's left with a shell of an identity. It's not even him and you can understand how devastating it can be not to know who you are anymore.

"I think this is particularly dangerous because I think

most men get more of a sense of their identity through work than any other avenue. Work is tied to financial rewards, supporting your family, your title and rank, if you're Associate, Vice-President, or Partner, it brings you into a certain league. You can feel you're important, that you've made it. You have a special label or title now and you identify with your company. For most men, it's where they spend the bulk of their time so it becomes more and more of who they are. But no matter how hard you try, it's hard to distinguish between your role at work and who you really are. This is a complicated issue.

"Creative work, creative arts would allow a man more expression of who he really is. But the real antidote to all this is to realize that your life is more important than your job. Never be pressured at work to take on something you don't really want or believe in, or that runs contrary to who you are. Even if it's a million dollar client, I won't take it if I don't like the person. Stick with your own values in these matters, if you can."

Alan has pinpointed a problem that is wider and broader than we imagine. The loss of one's real self, and confusion of identity becomes apparent in many men, especially when their jobs are at risk, or when they reach retirement. There are also large numbers of men who use their relationships at work to replace a personal social life. Workaholics, of course, are the most intense example of this. Work and the rewards it seems to bring replace many aspects of living and relating, and keeps them from having to face intimacy and the "internal journey" they do not wish to make.

Discussing men and work, Leslie Malin, MSW, Executive Coach and expert in Career Transition Consulting said,

"Men are extremely identified with their jobs in terms of who they are in the world and how they perceive themselves as breadwinners and supporters for their family. We see this especially in the case of a loss of a job. It's a huge blow to a man's sense of identity, security and safety in the world. When men are precluded from generating results they feel they've lost their worth and are often adrift and frightened.

"Many men that I've counseled who had lost their jobs had some kind of ongoing salary for a time, so they could go for awhile without acknowledging to their spouses what had happened. Here they were, carrying this sense of loss, and failure and also fear of telling their spouses. Many never even gave their spouses a chance to be supportive, there was so much shame involved. It is necessary, of course, to help a man deal with issues of shame, help him mourn the job that was lost, and the sense of identity that was lost with it. You help him find the courage to ask his wife and family for support.

"A lot of the focus of counseling is asking the men to step back and take a look at what they really lost. When they're able to stand back and separate their sense of identity from the job they begin to look at whether or not the job is really what they want in their life, is it expressing who they really are? They often find it isn't. Some are able to suddenly see that being fired could be one of the greatest gifts they were given. It allows them not to redefine their work, but to redefine themselves. What it is they really love to do, and how do they want their future to look? Most of us don't have the time to stand still long enough and look at that."

To many men doing the work they love seems a luxury, something to be saved for the later years. To others it seems impossible. For most this question never even arises. They have no idea what they really love, never having been trained to think that way. The work they choose is either based upon the financial rewards it will bring, or upon a need for status and identity, the role it will allow them to portray.

For some, work itself is a way to blot out other aspects of their lives. It is a way to hide from themselves the fact that they have never stopped to find out what they love, what they need and who they really are.

Living to Work—Workaholicism

"It's easy to fall into workaholicism," William, the father of three said through tightly pursed lips. Stopping for a few moments in his harried day, he brushed the papers on his desk aside and sank into his leather chair. "I have exactly fifteen minutes for this," he said.

"I'm doing it because it's a favor a friend of mine asked me to do."

William said it was hard to take fifteen minutes to be interviewed because, "I'm an enormously busy man. Everybody wants a piece of me, but I have work to do. Work comes first. It has to."

William has always been this way. "How do you think I got where I am? Sitting around twiddling my fingers, or holding my wife's manicured hand? I give her everything she could dream of—the house, rings, money, the kids, two cars, great vacations, whatever she needs."

William can give her everything but himself. "I'm happier here in the office," he said, "and she's better off without me at home. I'm there enough, for things that turn up. A person can't have everything."

Clearly William is using his work to escape from many other aspects of life, from intimacy, being with his family, or from the hurt and inadequacy he may feel inside. For him, success and money are compensations for everything.

"The wife gets more than most," William kept repeating, "just look at her closets."

William wasn't able to explain what he was getting though, and when the interview was over he dove deep into the papers on his desk.

Many men are in the grip of workaholicsm, a drug which provides a sense of power, adequacy and the ability to provide all that is needed of them. It blocks out other needs and longings. Often these men have no idea about how to experience closeness, relaxation, peace of mind, or to provide the greatest gift of all—themselves.

When the Work Cycle Ends

After their working days come to a close, we can see the fruits that the years of work have brought to men. Have they ripened into wise men and mentors? Do others seek out their succor and guidance? Has their work brought the kind of fulfillment they now need as they face the later years? Unfortunately, in the cases of men who have not developed hobbies, friendships or other interests during the work years, there is little left to sustain them. After retirement they have no further purpose. Usually the wife has a busy life. She continues her activities with children, grandchildren, and others, but life has changed very radically for these post-workaholic men. Even though they've worked hard, they have developed workships—not friendships. The loneliness they experience with the end of work can be very hard to bear.

Unfortunately, in our culture the later years for men are the most difficult in many ways. When the work cycle ends many feel tossed aside. They are considered useless, without position, value or dignity. Upon retirement, many regress, using their time to play games, take vacations and wander around. For some this free time was thought to be a reward for working many years. However, the bare reality of this experience can be devastating. Rather than having these later years be a culmination of a lifetime of experience where they are highly valued and regarded, there is a sense of loss of self-worth and of identity. In our youth-worshipping culture, older men are viewed as dispensable, both in the work force and in life in general. If the man has not acquired a strong sense of identity apart from his work and social status, this time of life can be so painful that many grow ill and die early.

What Was It All For?

Phil, a sixty-seven-year-old man who retired one year ago from a thriving business he started from scratch said,

"I'm depressed and I feel worthless. I don't understand what it was all about. I worked hard. Now time hangs heavy on my hands. I had a big business, had lots of money and prestige. I'm still a consultant with my business, but don't feel wanted there. All those years I was so important, when everybody was hanging on every word and now, I'm not wanted. I wonder what was my life really about? I made enough to send my kids to school and they're all living in different parts of the country and I don't even see my grandchildren. I've got to make an appointment to see them and I don't even feel they're that interested in seeing me. I have another daughter who's gay, and a son who says he'll never get married. I've seen it all. Now I've become cynical. Now I'm depressed too. I did what I had to do. Never owed anyone a nickel. Made money, sent my kids to school. They all had a nice place to live. My wife had nice clothes. We did some travelling. We had some friends. I guess that's all life is. But it's over. What do I have now? Arthritis. I had a little scare with cancer. I'm not getting any healthier. My wife is sick. What is there to look forward to? Getting older?"

These vital questions that Phil is now asking need to be asked and answered continually throughout a man's life. What's it all for? Where am I going? What am I getting and giving out of this?

Now that work responsibilities are gone, there's an opportunity for Phil to start a new life. When it was mentioned to him that now he has the time to do all the things he's always wanted to do, he shrugged. "Like what?" he said. "Ah, I'm all played out. All my life I just thought I had to prove something. So, I proved it. So what?"

Phil proved that he was the kind of man that society asked him to be. He didn't take time to find out who he truly was, or spend time doing that which was meaningful to him. Some men blame their responsibilities for this, saying they didn't have time. This is an excuse. When something is important, the time to do it can be found. If men realized how crucial it was to make time throughout the years, for that which is meaningful to them, their later years would feel fruitful, not empty.

It is a serious mistake to put this off. When interests and hobbies have not been nourished over time, to the man's distress, none are present later on when they're needed. The life in him has gone. His soul has become dry. Like a bank account filled with reserves that can be drawn upon later, what we give time and energy to throughout our lives will accumulate in richness as we grow older. If nothing has been put into the bank account, there will be nothing to draw upon.

The True Self

The belief or illusion that we can prove our worth as human beings by our work, accomplishments and the money we make, is a strong illusion that many live by. It is like a drug which clouds the consciousness and produces a feeling of well-being, while underneath the truth goes unattended to. While work and the accomplishments can have great value, there is a deeper need, to live from, and grow the True Self who resides within. Work that comes out of true being never leaves anyone feeling bereft and alone. The great work that must be done by all, no matter what his occupation, is to find and feed the True Self, the fountain of richness and aliveness within.

A beautiful old poem by Wang We, a Taoist, speaks of an entirely different way to think of life and of work. It speaks to us of "non doing," which is not laziness or procrastination, but the ability to be simple and humble, to have a new sense of our place in the world, and let life do its work through us.

> *"In the old days, the serious man was not an important person.*
> *He thought making decisions was too complicated for him.*
> *He took whatever small job came along.*
> *Essentially, he did nothing, like these walnut trees."*
> —*Wang We*

Touchstones to Remember

1. There are both "external" and "internal" warriors, men who need to conquer external obstacles and challenges, and those who need to find the truth of

who they are within. For a balanced life, a man must be able to be both of them.

2. Men need to find their ultimate challenge, personal quest, and let their work express it.

3. There are workships and relationships. Men must be aware of the difference between them and be sure they cultivate both.

4. It is crucial for men never to allow work, and the demands it imposes, to cause them to forget about the quality of their personal relationships.

5. Loneliness and coldness arise from living from a "false self." Men must remember that they are never the role they play at work, or anywhere else.

6. Work is a part of life—men must be careful not to drown in it and use it to hide from important relationships.

7. *What is it all for?* This is a question that must be asked and answered continually, throughout the years. Men must keep aware of what they are receiving and giving, the true meaning their work has for all.

8. Hobbies and interests must be cultivated throughout a man's life. He must not postpone doing that which is truly interesting and meaningful to him, or when the time comes for doing it, there will be no interests left to enjoy.

FIVE

Men and Their Friendships

The deep importance of male friendship cannot be over-emphasized. Some men are blessed with the ability to have male friendships that are deep, enduring and a source of comfort and support in their lives. These men are in the minority. Many men have no idea how to make this happen. Their relationships with other men revolve around sports, work, and competition. Close, personal, intimate time shared with a "buddy" is absent from their lives. The toll this takes upon these men is enormous, and in some cases emulates the closeness they never had, and always longed for, with their fathers.

Male friendship requires trust of another male and also sufficient personal security to let down the "male image" some men feel forced to play. A man must be able to admit his human needs and vulnerability in order to establish a friendship.

Personal Inventory: Men and their Frienships

Group A: Warriors, Heroes, Adventurers
Group B: Lovers, Dreamers, Peter Pans
Group C: Controllers, Perfectionists, Addicts
Group D: Wise Men, Gurus, Seers
Group E: A Real Guy!

SCORING
(Score each question from 1–4 in the following manner)

1. Not at all
2. Sometimes
3. Often
4. All the time

1. How good was his relationship with his father?

2. How important are male friendships to him?

3. Is his wife or partner the one he confides in most?

4. Is he always fighting with a boss or superior at work?

5. Does he always want to be out there, doing something?

6. How much does he enjoy a quiet night at home, one-on-one with someone?

7. How good does he feel about himself as a man?

8. How many hobbies and activities has he kept or developed as the years have gone by?

9. How able is he to be vulnerable?

10. How much does he feel he has to protect his image of himself as "strong"?

11. Does he plan social activities well?

12. Is he the life of the party?

13. How competitive is he with other men?

14. How much does he trust others?

15. How important are gender differences to him in his relationships?

16. Does he depend on [certain friends for his life] and only stay with them?

17. How many old friends has he maintained from years gone by?

18. Does he demand a great deal from his friendships and reject them if they let him down?

19. Is he open to becoming close with new people all the time?

20. Does he view the world as containing no strangers, only friends he hasn't yet met?

ANSWERS

Group A: Warriors, Heroes, Adventurers
(Questions 1, 5, 8, 10) Score 12 points or more

These men often have had strong male role models and sturdy relationships with their fathers. They have intense masculine identifications and enjoy being involved in activities and projects with other men. Their bonding comes about through taking action, and doing things together. The strongest friendships they develop arise out of a common mission.

Group B: Lovers, Dreamers, Peter Pans
(Questions 3, 6, 9, 12) Score 12 points or more

These men often find the closest friendships with their wives or lovers. They are able to be open and vulnerable and enjoy quiet, intimate time spent together. Other men are often seen as rivals for the loved one, and close friendships with men can be cursory. For many of these men love and friendship are one.

Group C: Controllers, Perfectionists, Addicts
(Questions 4, 13, 18, 16) Score 12 points or more

Friendships are most difficult for men in this group as they are so preoccupied with having power and control over another that the trust, closeness and intimacy required is usually out of their reach. These men are often lonely for male friendships, but feel they live in a dog-eat-dog world, where men compete with one another and are not able to really be friends.

Group D: Wise Men, Gurus, Seers
(Questions 14, 16, 19, 20) Score 12 points or more

These men live a life of friendship, seeing themselves as the ultimate friend to all of the world. They do not distinguish one group from another, but look for the commonality in all beings, and look for that which is to be admired and cherished in everyone.

Group E: A Real Guy!
(Questions 2, 7, 11, 17) Score 12 points or more

Friendships are important to these men and they are willing to work hard to make them happen. They are loyal, dependable and feel good about themselves, and can therefore risk disappointment and rejection, which can be a part of all relationships. They are willing to take the lead, make calls and plan social activities to maintain the friendships that are important to them.

Losing Male Friends after Marriage

Some men suddenly discover after a period of being married that they have lost their old friends, and now are living a life their wives have created for them. Seth, an attractive engineer, in his early forties said,

"One day I realized all our friends were the friends that my wife made. We have two small children and she's home taking care of them, spending time with other women, so it's easier for her to do this. These women all get together, and sooner or later, drag their husbands along. A group of couples develop, and you're part of it, whether you like it or not. The guys are out working most of the day, and don't relate to each other like that.

"Most of the men I meet through these couples, I'm not particularly interested in. They're not my choice, and, I guess, I'm not their choice either, but no one does anything about it. No one feels they can pursue a friendship with a guy out of the group. Who has the time?"

Seth has become submerged in his marriage and the group of couples that have developed around it. He has lost both his individuality and ability to choose to spend time with guys of his own liking.

My Wife Is My Best Friend

"Also," Seth continued, "my wife is my best friend. This has disadvantages, because there are things I can't tell her. She gets upset about things that I don't think are that important, so I don't tell her. If I'm worried about something on the job, she doesn't have to know.

"Besides that, there are plenty of ways she and I are different. For one thing my wife is interested in shopping, clothes, hair, nails, fashion magazines and stuff like that. I'm not interested in that at all. When she gets together with other women, that's what she talks about. She laughs and has a good time, but it's not part of my world. I've let go of all of my old friends, or they're in different parts of the country, doing different things, and I feel isolated."

When one person has to fulfill every role in another's life, this demand can be too great. We all need a variety of individuals to whom we can relate. Seth and many men like him are deprived of this.

"I also can't tell her that sex isn't so great anymore," Seth continued. "At the beginning it was okay, it was more than okay. But then when the kids came it changed. And she seems to be fine without it. If I had a real male friend I'd talk about that, I'd tell him she can go about two weeks without having sex and that's not enough for me. I think about sex all the time. I know other guys do too. I'd like to talk about it with them. I don't know who I am anymore. I used to play ball when I was a kid with other guys, but they're someplace else now and I don't have time for that."

A large part of Seth's identity, which is formed by his position with peers in a male group, has been lost in this lifestyle arrangement. He knows himself as a father and husband, but his experience of being one of the "guys" is absent. Seth does try to find time for himself, he said,

"Occasionally, if I want to break away, or want to have some time to myself, I go to a local bar. And I don't have anything much in common with these guys. But, I watch the ball game and we laugh a little. I come home drunk. I have to go to work the next day, so that's not satisfying, that's not what I'm looking for. I'd like to have a couple of buddies I can do things with, go on a fishing trip for a couple of days, or cross the mountains, or do some hiking. When I mention it to my wife she says, 'Why can't we do that together as a family?' We can do that together as a family, but it's not the same, because I'm tied into all the things of the family when I'm with her. I'm not just me."

Being "Just Me"

This need to be "just me" is a strong need for all. Seth has to stay in touch with his own selfhood to be able to grow as a husband, father, and as himself. Jung refers to this as the precious need all human beings have to individuate, to become more of who they are. All individuals require the time and space to be themselves, separate from their relationship, job, or group of friends. Only then can they have new and fresh contributions to make. Only then can they have and develop a strong connection with their inner selves.

A way out of this dilemma for Seth is,

"Well, I could bury myself in work. I could work sixty hours a week, make more money and not have to think about anything else, but I don't want to do that. I used to be a musician and I like music. I play the violin—maybe I could get together in some kind of little string quartet. Maybe I could find a group of guys who play other instruments and we could get together. It takes a lot of energy to do this though, and it takes a lot of time. After my family and work responsibilities are taken care of, believe me, there's not much left,"

Seth sounds as though returning to music is just a vague dream, not something he will actually make happen. He seems tired and played out, with a resigned passivity about him. He is harboring a sense of himself as a victim, someone who's been used and abused by the system. In order to get out of a situation like this, strong determination is needed as well as outside support, particularly the support of other men.

"I'm not crazy about this modern life of couples," Seth continued. "I don't see any real benefits to it. I know when I grew up, my father used to have loads of male friends. They used to go fishing together, play cards. My mother had her thing, she entertained women during the day. My parents didn't spend a lot of time together, not as much as my wife wants me to spend with her. My wife wants me to be her friend, instead of her husband. My father and mother got along okay, but they weren't really friends, not like my wife and me. My parents each had their own friends, and did things together on family occasions and holidays.

"The expectation today is that couples should be best friends and do everything together. I think it's a mistake. If I had a choice and could start over, I wouldn't get married young again. I was twenty-two when I got married. Maybe

I wouldn't get married at all. I'd travel more. I wouldn't want to live in a suburban area like I do now, and have the responsibility of children. Maybe when I got older. I'd take a lot of time for freedom and exploration. And I'd make sure I had my friends. I'm not too satisfied with this set-up. I don't know where it's going either. I'm going to stay in it until the kids are grown. We get along well enough, but there's no spark."

Living on Top of a Time Bomb

Seth's marriage is built on top of a time bomb. Seth is passing his time passively, nursing his wounds and feeling deprived. Sooner or later, probably when the children get older, this resentment will come to the surface and he'll take off, leaving a dazed wife behind.

When a man feels powerless to get his needs met in a situation, and powerless to have the time with male friends he deeply craves, a boomerang is inevitable. There is no one person to blame—responsibility for this situation lies in Seth's corner as well. For starters, he needs to open up and communicate about his dissatisfaction to his wife. He also needs to seek other outlets for his desire for friendship. Rather than threaten the marriage, outside interests or activities could save it in the long run if both Seth and his wife understood the gravity and depth of his feelings, the need for male friendship, and for individuation—to be himself.

A Man Wants to Be Able to Talk to Another Man

Alex, an account executive in his late thirties, living in Manhattan and raised in the West, agrees how important it is for men to have close friends.

"A man needs to be able to talk to another man and ask how he can deal with different problems that arise. No matter what his age, he wants someone to ask 'What do I do?' Most men don't have friends like they used to and it's hard to find somebody who's going through what they're going through at a particular time. I keep all my old friends like diamonds in my pocket. Here's an example—a good friend from the West called me a couple of years ago and said, 'Listen, you know I've been married a long time and it's been all right, but now I have something else going too, and it's turned into more than I can handle. It's driving me crazy. What should I do?'

"I was pleased and proud he called me to ask. So, the two of us took three days off, went fishing, and talked about the situation the whole time. We talked about every side of it, with nothing left out. After those three days he went home, cleaned up his act and went back to his wife and family. That really made me feel good. He told me he guessed he just needed a good friend to talk to. Nothing like it. I felt I made a big difference. The time we had together was fantastic—something both of us needed too."

Unfortunately most men don't have someone who would do that for them. Alex explained,

"Most don't have real buddies anymore. Thank God he and I are close. My friends are so important to me, but it doesn't always work out this way. I had another guy who I thought was my best friend and I brought him into my business and he cheated me. Now he's not my friend at all. That can happen too. You never know how long a friendship will hold up. But when things go bad, lots of guys give up on everyone after that."

Because most men do not have the experience of communicating their hurt, or other personal feelings to one another, when a relationship goes bad, they withdraw and nurse their wounds. It is often hard for them to trust again, not having understood or worked out what went on before.

Alex is a wonderful example of someone with an old-fashioned male friendship that is so sadly lacking for many today. Some men are stopped by their need to maintain a certain image, or by fear of being exposed, revealed for who they are. Distrust of themselves is what keeps them separate from others.

No Male Relationship He'd Ever Felt Comfortable With

Philip, a very attractive, successful man in his sixties, spent years as the CEO of a major company, raised a family, and is regarded highly in his community. Despite all the external signs of success, he feels lonely now, deeply missing and craving the male bonding and support he felt he never had.

"There isn't a male relationship that I ever felt comfortable with," Philip said. "It's a matter of degree, there are some men that I feel more at ease with, but basically there's some profound mistrust in me so that I never truthfully reveal who I am to other men.

"Naturally, I've thought about this a great deal and attribute it to my relationship with my father, but it's not something I feel a visceral truth about. I just feel logically that's where it has to be. I can easily see if my father had been a warm, easy person who made it okay for me to be the way he was, then that's how I'd be. But that's not the kind of guy he was. He seemed to me to be remote, he wasn't around, he wasn't easily approachable, I had very few experiences involving intimacy with him. We didn't hang out together, he didn't teach me very much. And also he was an authority figure with a lot of leverage in the house, so I automatically endow all male figures with that. It immediately stops me from being open or at ease with them."

Relationship with the Father

One of the basic precepts of modern psychology is that the way a boy relates to other men is deeply affected by the nature of his relationship with his father, and with his ability to identify with him, to accept the model of manhood the father presents. Philip's father was a successful businessman, so in that respect, Philip did identify with him. His father was also unable to be open, or relate closely to other men, and in this respect as well, Philip has emulated his style. But the deep fear he had of his father, and the sense that there was no room for him in the family to be who he was, created a life-long chasm between Phillip and other men.

Who Am I in the Eyes of Other Guys?

"There are circumstances under which I do relate comfortably," Philip continued, "one particularly has to do with sports. When I'm playing ball, I'm totally comfortable with the other guys. Actually, when I'm playing all of these issues don't exist becaues I'm so focused on the need to be connected, which is what sports is all about. In order for the team to accomplish its objectives, you have to be linked to each other in a certain way. That's why I like team sports. I don't like individual sports, like skiing or tennis. I particularly enjoy team sports because then I'm very aware of making a contribution, and I also love the acknowledgment of all the other men on the team."

Sports has become an acceptable arena for Philip to get his needs for closeness to other men met. Here he is finally able to feel acknowledged and validated. There is a down side to that as well, as Philip clearly states.

"Naturally," he continued, "if you do well, the experience is totally different than if you do poorly. You can feel totally exhilarated or totally crushed. I'm very affected by how I see myself in the eyes of the guys, by how I'm doing. I'm a very, very competitive person. My relationships are based upon a win-lose impulse, it's a primeval thing."

Ending Up the Loser

Many men relate to one another on a win-lose basis. In Philip's case, he said,

"It's always in the air because I'm always concerned that I'm going to end up a loser if I'm not on my guard, and defending myself. This can happen in sports or in social relationships. If I get blindsided somehow and open myself up, and then get made a fool of, or have my trust violated, that's murder for me. It happens plenty too. For example, if I'm saying something, and someone gets angry, that shuts me down immediately. I feel that my urge to be mistrustful has been validated. This tends not to happen in a business context, because there I have the authority and feel in control."

Philip cannot handle either his anger or the anger of others toward him, except when it's channeled into business or sports. The minute pure anger arises, he withdraws and feels he can't trust. In truth, what he cannot trust are his own feelings, or his ability to handle them. In this case it is extremely important for him to learn that anger need not be deadly. It can be experienced directly and expressed appropriately. He is not a loser, nor is his value as a person wiped out if someone becomes angry with him.

Many individuals have little understanding or experience in dealing with their anger, or recognize the toll it takes in every area of their lives. If Philip could become more at home with his anger, he would become more at home with others as well.

Dr. Diane Shainberg addresses anger when speaking of what prevents men from sharing who they are and being open in relationships.

> "What many men have to hide," she said, "is their hideous need for revenge. When you have a person who's been hurt by his parents not liking him, being close to him, or even seeing or hearing his precious being, you can have enough hurt so that there is a strong desire for revenge. Although men can take revenge through sports or business, I think the thing they hide more than anything else is this hatred, this desire to be aggressive and hurt back. The aggressiveness is the defense against their hurt, but revenge can go so deep that we become afraid of it, and for that reason, we hide."

"My observation," Philip continued, "is that relatively few men have close relationships with other men. There are a significant number of exceptions to that, but it's a relatively small minority."

While men were parented by a wide range of fathers, Philip believes all men have difficulty connecting, "Because all had fathers who were authority figures—calling all the shots. This created certain reactions when their sons were particularly vulnerable."

Being the Authority Figure

According to Phillip, as long as the father is a strong authority figure, the son has no chance of feeling comfortable or growing in a way he needs to. In fact now, in order to be comfortable with other men, Phillip must play the authority role himself. In this way he becomes his father, and turns other men into who he was, the uneasy son. As the father in the interaction, he is always on top. Needless to say, this paradigm could never produce the warmth, closeness and intimacy Phillip hungers for.

Unfortunately, Philip thinks that the authority role of the father can't be reversed. Philip said,

"It's almost impossible, because the father's coming out of who he is and he can't change who he is even if he's inclined to do it. I think he can up to a point, but it's very limited and the question is, how far you can modulate it. So this behavior just keeps getting passed down the generations. I mean, if you go to work on yourself and you get a lot of that work done before your kids are at a certain age, you can modify who you are up to a point. I've done it probably more than most men have, particularly with my children, my sons and my daughter. But, I think in my own mind, there are many things I would have liked to have done with my sons that I didn't do. All the kinds of things that I would have liked my father do with me."

There's a term coined by Robert Bly called Father Hunger. This describes a man's hunger to have a father he can be close to, identify with, even look upon as a hero. It is a hunger also to become that man oneself. When the father is absent in the family, this hunger can't be satisfied and in some cases dominates a man's entire life. In Philip's case there seems to be a great deal of father hunger because of the kind of relationship he had with his father. This caused both his need for closeness and fear of it.

"There were a couple of figures in my life," Philip continued, "who played a father role to me. I never forgot them. One was a guy who was my baseball coach years ago, where it was really a father-son relationship. He was particularly warm. There was also a guy who lived at our house in Chicago for about six months. I guess he was working for my father and needed a place to live—I don't know what the circumstances were—but he was the one who taught me to drive. It was the first experience I'd had on a continuing basis of warm, generous, caring from a man. I loved it. I never forgot it."

This is a testimony to how deep the need is for warm caring from the father as well as the mother. Fathers who simply play the role of stern authority figures may, inadvertently, be depriving their sons of much-needed strength.

In considering the cultural impact on relationships between men Philip said,

"The only culture which it seems to me that there is a difference in how men relate to one another that I'm aware of is the Italian culture. The men appear to be very much at ease with each other. They're generously open with their emotions, they're physically at ease with one another, do a lot of hugging, and putting their arms around each other. It seems very natural and to be part of the culture."

Despite his feelings of being isolated, Philip has lived a life of interaction with men through business, sports, lunches, meetings, etc. but found only a certain level of dissatisfaction in them.

"I think of these men as business friends," he said. "Some few are personal friends, just a few. In terms of my feelings about them, I'm close to them. But if you define closeness as spending a lot of time, and doing things together, no. You go through different phases of life though. There were periods of time when it seemed I had close relationships, when I hung out with guys, but then one day they disappeared. They went one way and I went another. This is not a part of life that I've ever adapted to. I mean people will work here for about five years, ten years, or whatever, and then they decide to go, and just go. I feel a separation. I ask myself how it can be that two people could spend ten years together intensely involved in all kinds of situations where you support one another and go through various things, and then they're just gone—never look back. It's shocking."

Without relationships that endure over time there is always the experience of loss and separation, of people coming and going, not looking back. While the family unit used to provide that consistency, sadly today, families, too, are constantly separating.

Male Intimacy

Phillip is aware that he must take responsibility to make relationships grow.

"First of all I don't think anybody has more than four or five close friends at any particular time. Close friends are very time-consuming, a major commitment. So, it's a matter of degree.

"I guess you have to do what friends do to become friends. In part it is up to me, in part the geography has to work as well. And then in business there are certain things that are appropriate, and certain that are not. A lot can get in the way.

"Basically, it's probably my discomfort with intimacy. I don't really know how, beyond a certain level. I can play baseball with a guy every day, because I'm not sitting across a table relating to him and having conversations. And, in the business sense I'm protected, because everybody knows what their roles are. It's not about intimacy. Also, in the business setting I'm in a position of authority which feels like a protection I have an invisible wall around me that keeps me from being invaded in certain ways."

Philip is deeply at the mercy of his own fear of sharing his personal feelings and exposing who he is. He lacks a feeling of safety with men, expecting to be judged or attacked. He also has a great need to be in charge, viewing all relationships as win-lose. On the other hand, he longs for closeness with other males. In order to attain this closeness, he would have to relinquish some of his defenses, be who he is, and trust that the other was not out to get him, but had basic good will. He, too, would have to develop his own sense of acceptance and good will toward other men. For men living in such a competitive mode, this is difficult. While they may win for a long time and be in command, the price they pay for this is essential loneliness.

Kill or Be Killed

"There's something about competition that doesn't seem to be escapable. If you think about it for a minute I've been raised in sports from a very early age, and in sports you spend hours and hours, days, months, years, seeing how close you can come to killing somebody without doing it. So, if you're on a team with a bunch of other killers you have some protection, and you can go out and get rid of all that in-grained aggressiveness. If you're more successful than some-body else, you're better. It's kill or be killed here. You suffer for it though, in every way, not only physically, but also emotionally."

Clearly a huge block to intimacy is the aggression Philip and other men live with, and the fear that it will come back at them. In another sense, aggression itself is a form of inti-macy, of becoming entangled and close. Philip doesn't seem to realize that he continues to choose and hold onto this way of being, that there are men who do not interact with one another this way.

"The way I experience it," Philip continued, "is a matter of survival. It's not like I want to be an angry, aggressive guy, I just want to keep living. Aggressiveness is such a big part of our culture. Business, for instance, everyone is shafting everyone else. We're living in a dog-eat-dog world. Every-one becomes your opponent. Especially when you get into a position of authority in business as you climb the ladder, it becomes increasingly impossible to be honestly open. I'm speaking of being emotionally open—you just can't do it, because being successful is the primary objective of being in business."

The time Philip feels most comfortable with other men is when he feels secure at work, with plenty of money. He said,

"Even though I know this is a lousy solution—the time I felt most comfortable being closer with guys was when I felt unthreatened, when I felt secure that my job or livelihood would not disappear. Then I felt strong, on top of the particular world I was in.

"When I had plenty of money at one point, I didn't feel threatened because if someone misbehaved, it didn't matter, because I felt I had lots of options. Actually having money made it seem as though the need to have intimate relationships with men was unnecessary. Now I realize that the money and sense of security at work that I had was just a drug."

At this point in his life Philip recognizes that leaning on money and position for a sense of value and security only works up to a point. It does not provide the real, inner security, sense of worth, and closeness he needs at this point in his life. By feeling lonely and insecure at this point in his life, Philip is actually receiving an opportunity to grow, to face and dissolve his inner fears so that he can attain the closeness with other men he so longs for.

Changing the Way Men Relate to One Another

Philip wishes something could be done to change the ways men relate to one another.

"There may very well be other ways of living than what I've experienced," he said, "I guess the way out of it is through comprehension on as profound a level as one is able to achieve. The way you do that is to put yourself into circumstances where you can raise your consciousness into what it means to be alive—workshops like The Forum, Loving Relationships, whatever it is that works for you, so you learn as much about who you are and what matters to you as possible.

"Also, somebody ought to set up a training program for fathers. That's where it has to start. Someone has to put some balance into young men's training and eliminate the unbridled competitive aspect of it, but I think it's impossible. I am sure this is connected to the violence among kids. If you just go into the toy store and just look at the games for boys and for girls. It blows your mind away."

At whatever point in the age continuum, men need to learn a variety of ways of relating to each other, gaining status and position, and understanding what it truly means to be strong. This comes not only from their relationship with their fathers and family, but from peers, and values taught in schools. New role models are crucial, models that males can respect, as a step toward knowing and respecting themselves.

Male Mentors

Mentors have the potential to make a difference in young men's lives. Philip agreed, "That guy in my house made a big impact on me because of who he was. It's who the person is that makes one hundred percent of the difference."

In the interviews with kids who kill, they said almost across the board that there was just no one there, no one home to listen to them. The communication gap between generations is huge. Ironically, the more global communication we have, the less human contact. It's the human contact that Philip and many young men in his position now crave. Mentoring by elders is a wonderful way to address that need. By helping others who are disconnected and experiencing the same pain, you see that you're not alone in the situation and that your painful experiences can now be used to help others, they were not all for nothing. We must draw on the resources that we have developed from our life experiences. If we do, and share these experiences with others, we will feel needed, productive, and valuable no matter what happened in the past.

Men Who Care about Other Men

Dan Foley, a successful estate planner and financial investment advisor in his mid-fifties has spent years dedicated to working with other men and with himself in understanding men's needs and how to build truly satisfying friendships. He's led many groups for men on male consciousness-raising dealing with these issues.

"I had a job for awhile in men's groups, where I greeted the new men and helped integrate them into the organization," Dan said, "so I got to know a lot of men. About ninety percent of the men who came to us are joining fraternal organizations, which by the way, are growing enormously because there's a huge hunger in American men for male companionship, and for men who care about other men, and their well-being. The fraternal organizations are very protective of their members and of what they're doing because male bashing goes on so much, and is so commonly a part of our culture today, that people don't even realize they're doing it. When Bly, (Robert Bly, author of *Iron John*), began his work in Minnesota and put on men's conferences he was subject to enormous ridicule. What does that say about how men feel about themselves today? With those feelings how can they have real friendships?"

Positive Male Models

"We have so few models left. I was lucky in a way, I grew up in a home with my grandparents. I knew them very well as a boy. I loved them very much and saw that there were defined areas in their lives. My grandfather was a classic self-made man, both in business and in an emotional sense. He was an orphan, and my grandmother was also an orphan. They came from a little town in Michigan that their families had founded, and they were farm people, basically. My grandfather became an attorney and went to Notre Dame. I inherited his name and lots of things from him, including his spirit, with certain differences too. He was your classic tough guy, a prosecuting attorney most of his life, and he was tough. He was loving, but he was tough. I knew him well enough to know I was glad he wasn't my father. My father had it tough with him. But that's the old-type fathering that is so controversial today."

Dan is especially fortunate to have had male role models that spanned the generations, and especially a strong figure he could respect, relate to and identify with. His ability to have friends and relate warmly to other men was positively influenced by the men in his life.

A Father Needs to Be a Father

"Today we've got a lot of fathers who are their sons' friends and that's not bad," Dan continued, "but there's also a point at which the father needs to be a father. I'm not sure he always does his son a service if he's not fairly tough with him. This helps the son learn what it means to be a strong man. I think we've got a lot of passivity in men, a lot of softness. What we've got is men who are leaving more and more of the fathering duties to the woman, and the male is becoming weaker and weaker in the bargain."

In a sense Dan is making a claim for the value of having a traditionally strong father in the home. He feels that young men crave this, and actually require it in order to get in touch with their own inner strength. The absence of this is felt as abandonment by many younger men.

"I'm aware it is not politically correct to say that it's okay for a father to be tough—I don't mean abusive. Now, my father on the other hand, reacted to his father and was a fairly soft father. He was not a tough guy and he had things go wrong in this life that made it difficult. He got ill early and his heart went out on him. He had problems that made him bitter as he got older, but I'll say this about my father, what I got from him affected my relationship with men. I'm very proud of the fact I have many intimate relationships with men friends. I go on a twice-yearly camping trip with men. We have monthly conference calls. I'm in touch with other men's lives."

Dan has made a focused effort to build and nurture his male relationships. They have been a source of ongoing support to him, and he is proud of his willingness to take time for this.

"If you talk with men and look at their lives, how they feel, what they've achieved, the men who've suffered the most, who have been the least able to accomplish the things they've wanted, are the men who have had the male bond broken, whose fathers did not give them some tough love or direction.

"What I admire about my father was that he never backed down. He never threw in the towel. He had the self-respect to fight for himself and he did not let himself be manipulated or controlled. Those were strong, positive qualities for which, I realize, I owe him a great deal."

Needing the Friendship of Men

Clearly, Dan internalized strong positive qualities from both his father and grandfather that made him able to develop, maintain and explore deep friendships with other men. Also, in his evaluation of these relationships, he has made a point of looking for the positive aspects of the relationships, what he got from them, rather than what he was deprived of. Some men never stop and ask themselves what was good about the relationship, what kind of lessons they may have learned. What strengths they internalized. There is a heavy judgment of and competitiveness with the father, sometimes with little compassion for what he went through himself. A broad view and lots of forgiveness are needed to see a relationship in its full context.

Dan thinks it was his relationship with his father and

grandfather that allowed him to have these intimate relationships with men.

> "But more than that, I wanted the male friendships. I was
> clear I needed them. One day I woke up and said, 'I need
> the friendship of men.' Most men don't make that admission,
> or know how to make it happen. What I did then was to
> explore workshops.

> "What I think has happened in America, because of the
> breakdown of so many old patterns, is the burgeoning in-
> dustry of workshops. There are all kinds of workshops
> around where you can deal with any issue you need to. I
> finally found one that filled the gap for me, and I created an
> ongoing support system out of it, a kind of a family. For the
> past ten or fifteen years to this day, this has continued. I
> know it has given me a lot more of a foundation and power
> in life."

In a sense these workshops, with their ongoing support
groups and meetings, also fill the function churches and synagogues have. People get together and explore what is meaningful to them, who they are, and what it really means to be
alive. Community and ongoing support is available. They are
not usually affiliated with a traditional religious faith and are
open to anyone regardless of ethnicity or background. Their
very purpose is to allow participants to express themselves
openly without fear of censor or repercussions.

Male Bonding

"There's a particular way men have of bonding and being
together that is different from how women bond," Dan said.
"What's happened today is that a lot of the models of how

relationships should happen are based upon a female model. I enjoy sitting around talking with the guys, but if that's all I do with them, it has limited appeal. But, if we go out and do a project together, make something happen, I love it. That's what a lot of the old, fraternal organizations used to do. Our group started a couple of non-profit corporations. There's a lot to do in the world and the power of the group is extraordinary. It really works for men to be involved in activity like this. It gives them pride. It's men doing what men do—creating things in the world. It's the only way that your time together isn't simply about competition. Join forces. Make a game out of it. This is how men operate."

By acknowledging the differences in the ways in which men and women bond, a woman can find new ways of developing intimacy with the man she is involved with. She can understand why he may not be able to sit with her in one room and talk for hours. By engaging in activities together, as well as spending time alone, the bond between them may deepen more easily.

Taking Care of the Wound from the Father

Men can accept the gift of the feminine—the ability to connect—only if they have

"addressed what it means to be a man," Dan continues. "If they have a wound from their father, they've got to take care of it. They can't pretend it's not there. For instance, I know a guy who just got out of one marriage, then dove into another relationship. That didn't work and so he dove into another. Now this guy's clearly got a father wound. His father was an abusive alcoholic and he's never done anything to heal that wound. He never addressed it, considered it, worked with it. He just said, 'Oh my father was a jerk.' He's never seen the affect this wound has in his life in lots of ways. Now he's becoming like his father in his relationships."

If you don't look at painful experiences in your life, heal them, come to terms with them, forgive the person and yourself, you are doomed to repeat these experiences in your life. You may also become just like the person you had most difficulty with. This is especially true for men who have wounds from the father, issues they have not yet come to peace with. It is well worth the time and energy needed to confront that primal relationship, see how it is affecting a man's life today, and make the repairs that are needed.

"I see that men wait and say, 'I'll take care of this father issue someday. I know it's a problem.' But these are the guys who, when they hit their fifties, go to pieces. I think the mind is not unlike the body. Lots of guys don't think twice about working out their body, keeping in shape. The same thing is true for the mind, and their spiritual lives. They've got to put something into themselves spiritually, and it's got to be real. They can't be just going through the motions of doing it. It's got to really hit home. They've got to get out there and allow themselves to expand, take in new information, be open. Then they can take that back to their lives and really have something."

Dan is an unusual and eloquent spokesman for being willing to look deeply into the nature of masculinity, what it means for him, help others do that, and put what he learned into action. It is necessary to have a strong determination to forge ahead in this direction, go against the stream, make friendships a priority, in order to create a life that is full and balanced in every way.

Touchstones to Remember

1. Men need friendship with other men outside of their marriage and group of couples. This is an arena in which different parts of themselves come alive. Without this, many men feel lonely and deprived.

2. Getting away alone with a buddy, going fishing, hiking, playing cards are deeply rejuvenating and also a way to work problems out. There are certain things that men can only discuss with another man.

3. A man's relationship with his father deeply affects his ability to be close to other men and have male friends.

4. There is considerable "father hunger" in many men. This is the lack of closeness, love, unconditional regard and acceptance by the authority in his life, the man he looks up to.

5. Many men find their identity and sense of self-worth in the eyes of other men and their peers. If they do not feel positively about themselves, this can profoundly affect their ability to establish male friends.

6. Constant competition with others, wondering who's going to win or lose, or who will kill or be killed, prevents the openness and mutual sharing needed for friendships.

7. Men who must be authorities or in control all the time live in prisons of their own making.

8. Male bonding is different from female bonding. Men need to "do" things together out in the world, create projects and feel effective.

9. In order to be able to accept "the gift of the feminine" a man must feel secure in himself and in his male relationships.

SIX

Men and Love

L ove was one of the most difficult areas to get men to talk about. "I can sleep with her, marry her, take care of her, but love—that's something else," said Tony, a married man in his late forties. "Guys don't like to talk about love. They don't know what to say. Of course guys do love. But they don't talk about it."

Still, women do not feel happy unless they hear those golden words: *I love you*. Men do not either. But as much as men want love, many fight it to the last minute. Love can make men feel vulnerable, childlike and unable to do what's expected of them—especially those who believe they're functioning in a dog-eat-dog world.

Personal Inventory: Men and Love

Group A: Warriors, Heroes, Adventurers
Group B: Lovers, Dreamers, Peter Pans
Group C: Controllers, Perfectionists, Addicts
Group D: Wise Men, Gurus, Seers
Group E: A Real Guy!

SCORING

(Score each question from 1–4, in the following manner)

1. Not at all
2. Sometimes
3. Often
4. All the time

1. Is he able to tolerate his feelings?

2. How good does he feel about himself as a man? Does he feel safe when he loves?

3. Does love seem turbulent to him, an impossible chase?

4. Does love seem to him to be more for women? Does it threaten his masculinity?

5. Would he rather have a night out with the boys then spend long hours with the person he loves?

6. How able is he to love, in general? Does he hold most of life in loving regard?

7. How much does he express his love daily in what he does?

8. Does he fall in love easily, and out of love just as easily?

9. Does he have to defend himself constantly, feeling that people can't really be trusted?

10. Does love feel like another mountain to conquer to him?

11. Does he feel that if you let yourself love, you are bound to get hurt and stepped on?

12. Is the ability to love one of the main goals of his life?

13. How hard is he willing to work for love? Is he willing to give a great deal?

14. Does life seem not worth living without love?

15. How good is he at compromise? Does he need to have all his needs met all the time?

16. Are love and fantasy intermingled for him? Can he tell the difference?

17. Does he feel that love is possession and attachment?

18. Are there many strings to his love? Is it too expensive?

19. Is he able to find love in the small moments of the day?

20. Do many people love him? Does he believe he deserves this?

ANSWERS

Group A: Warriors, Heroes, Adventurers
(Questions 3, 4, 5, 10) Score 12 points or more

These men see love as an obstacle course and enjoy the challenge it presents. They like to conquer women, and often feel as though the thrill is gone once she is his. These men create difficulties and intrigue in their relationships to keep them alive and challenging. Love is where they prove their prowess, not necessarily a place of intimacy.

Group B: Lovers, Dreamers, Peter Pans
(Questions 1, 8, 14, 16) Score 12 points or more

These men often view love as heightened romance, filled with poetry, dreams and peak experiences. They do not necessarily enjoy the daily work of sitting down and communicating about knitty gritty problems that arise. When too many problems appear, these men feel that love has gone. They want their feelings known magically, without saying a word.

Group C: Controllers, Perfectionists, Addicts
(Questions 9, 11, 17, 18) Score 12 points or more

For these men, love includes control and dominance. When their partner is willing to do as they wish, fulfill their needs, demands and fantasies, these men feel strong. When the partner expresses a mind or life of her own, they feel threatened, and as though the "love" is disappearing. These men confuse love with possession, attachment and dependency. They are afraid of equal, mutual relationships, where their inner selves will be exposed.

Group D: Wise Men, Gurus, Seers
(Questions 6, 12, 13, 19) Score 12 points or more

These men feel love for, and one with, the entire universe. They see love as the bond which connects all of life, and it is their main reason for living. For them love is the deep ability to heal, nourish, instruct and inspire. It does not necessarily have to include having a specific partner or mate.

Group E: A Real Guy!
(Questions 2, 7, 15, 20) Score 12 points or more

These men feel good about themselves and therefore feel safe enough to share themselves openly and express feelings. They make it a practice of expressing positivity in all aspects of their lives, of compromising and performing deeds of love throughout the day. Because they are usually giving, they feel deserving of love in return.

Saying I Love You

Actually saying the words, "I love you," is a huge step for some men. However, these words mean something different to each one, so it is important not only to listen to what is being said, but to see how love is being manifested in all aspects of the relationship.

"When I say 'I love you,'" said Steve, a stockbroker in his early thirties, "I feel like I'm taking my life in my hands and giving it to her. It's scary, like I'm giving her power over me. To be frank, I've only done this twice in my life, with my first girlfriend, and now with Naomi, the woman I'm engaged to. When I did it with my first girlfriend I was young, and didn't really know the difference. It was natural. We both said it at the same time. I thought the feeling would last forever. When it didn't, that really hurt. It took me a long time to get over it. With Naomi, it's different. I trust her. As our relationship goes on, it gets easier to say it every day."

Steve is describing how vulnerable some men feel when they actually tell a woman they love her. Just by saying it, they feel as though they are baring their souls, giving her the power to control or hurt them. For Steve, implicit in saying I love you, is also the hope that the love will last, and the fear of loss and failure if it doesn't. Before a man like Steve can say I love you, he must be able to trust a great deal.

For other men, like Burt, a salesman in his thirties, saying "I love you" is no big deal.

"I usually tell a woman I love her at about the fourth date," Burt said. "It's no big deal. They like to hear it, and I like to say it too. Once that hurdle has been passed it makes us closer. When a woman feels you love her, something in her relaxes. From that point on you can really find out who she is. It's easy for me to love women and to tell them so. It doesn't mean that much to me though—like saying 'I love you' doesn't mean I'm showing up one day with a ring."

For Burt love is casual, a way of naturally moving from one stage in a relationship to the next. It has no connotation of permanence, or commitment of any kind. "I believe you can love a lot of women," said Burt, "and I believe it is good to do so. When the one comes along who I'm going to marry, that will be different. I'll know right away who she is."

Burt was asked how he would know, and he smiled and said, "Because I'll really love that one."

Though Burt uses the word love in many situations, each time it has a different connotation for him. Burt, and other men like him, include all kinds of good feelings under the rubric of love: warmth, friendship, sexuality, and eventually commitment with one special one. It is important for a woman to understand what I love you means to the man she is hearing it from, and whether it matches what love means to her.

If You Really Love Someone
There's Not Much You Have to Say

Some men believe that love speaks for itself, there's not much they have to add. Jim, a handsome, rugged Italian man in his early fifties, laughed a little when he spoke about love.

"Well, if you really love someone, there's not much you have to say. The real feelings say it all. At my stage of the game, there's not too much I hold back. I think as you get older you don't want to miss any more opportunities to tell people how you care about them, what you think about them. But if it's real love, that's something else. They know it. They just do. When you're in a regular relationship with a woman at this stage of the game you don't say too much either, because you probably said those words once before. You feel silly saying them again and a lot of times you don't know if you're trying to convince that person or yourself. It's just much better to have the feelings between you, because those are honest. All the rest of the stuff, those fancy words come back to haunt you, and you've probably already been clubbed to death a thousand times with them anyhow."

When Jim, and men like him, are in love, they feel the women sense the strength of their feelings and automatically read their minds. This is a delicate situation, because intoxication, feelings of infatuation, fantasy and other emotions can be experienced as love. By not speaking of their feelings to the woman, these men are assuring that the relationship remains partially in the realm of fantasy. It is also a way of

preventing the relationship from deepening, and certainly in-
suring that the words don't come back to haunt them. True
commitment is held at bay. There is only so far a relationship
can go on the basis of silent understanding. Real issues, needs
and feelings inevitably arise and these must be discussed.

The Fact of the Matter Is We Are Love

Dan Foley, an estate planner in his mid-fifties, has a completely different take on love. He said,

> "The truth of the matter is that we are love. I am love. That's
> the fundamental acknowledgment we have to make. If we're
> not willing to make that acknowledgment about ourselves we
> can't make it to anybody in our lives. Because of the chang-
> ing nature of the roles between men and women this has
> become harder and harder for men to do these days."

For Dan, unless a man realizes that his very nature is love,
he will neither be able to either love another, nor express his
feelings naturally. Instead, he will always be looking for con-
firmation of who he is through the love relationship. This
seems dangerous to him, especially in today's world.

> "Lots of men are too scared to love, these days," he said.
> "There's so much fear in their lives right now, because the
> earth they stand on is shaky. So many things have been taken
> away from men these days, that it's scary to say that what I
> am is love. Most of the time it doesn't feel that way."

Dan is suggesting that the very ground of men's being has
been uprooted, causing them to be too preoccupied with security and their sense of identity to risk loving.

"Men's lives and identities aren't tied up with love these days. They're tied up with their incomes, how well they can compete and win. So much can go wrong with that so easily, that it's hard to be confident and tell a woman 'I love you,' because you never know what could go wrong tomorrow."

What Dan is actually saying is that in order to be able to love a man has to feel confident about who he is, has to succeed first in business, feeling good about his role vis a vis other men. When a woman looks at him and compares him to others, he must be confident that he will not fall short in her eyes. Until a man's identity is well established he may feel too fragile to risk asking for and offering love. Perhaps he may not feel he deserves it, has not earned the right to it yet. Or, he may fear that when another, more successful man, comes along, it will be easy for him to lure the woman away.

Love and Money

Dan doesn't think many men can love without the proper income.

"Because being successful with money is more of what makes a man who he is than having a successful love relationship. Men think they only have women in their lives because they're successful financially. They think that's what the women are after, that's what they really want. They don't know what else they can really offer her. I know now at my age that isn't true for all women. But most men don't realize it, it's hard for them to believe a woman will love them if they don't have enough money or status. That's why those things are so important to them."

Many men have identified their self-worth with their bank accounts. They do not feel desirable, or deserving of love unless they have earned it. Money and love are often confused, seen as supplies provided from the outside world, in acknowledgment of a man's value. That is why during the depression so many committed suicide when their financial worth disappeared. Without money, they felt worthless. Needless to say, this widespread confusion needs to be remedied in order for men to be able to open up to love. A man has to know who he is truly, what he deserves, and what he is capable of before he can commit to love. Eric Fromm speaks about the confusion between love and money.

"Modern man's happiness consists in the thrill of looking in shop windows and buying all he can afford. Love can be viewed in the same manner, by searching for an attractive man or woman, as a prize. These become human commodities. But love comes not to he who is rich, but he who gives much."

What's Frightening to a Man about Love

"Women are so much stronger," Dan said, "that it can be daunting to a guy. Women's lives today are the richest. There's more things possible than ever before. When I was in college Betty Friedan's book [*The Feminine Mystique*] came out. The women in my generation are the ones who changed the world. I don't know what percentage of women worked in my mother's generation, but now women are all over the workplace, in all kinds of jobs. The change is enormous—women have expanded their lives enormously. They don't need men the way they used to. That's terrifying for men today."

For Dan, and others like him, the desire to be needed by a woman is very strong. If she needs him, and he can take care of her, this provides him a sense of security in the relationship, a sense of having value. This man deeply needs to be valued by the woman he cares for, and if he doesn't feel this, the foundation of the relationship can be shaky.

"As my friend Robert Bly has said," Dan continued, "Men are getting softer and women are getting harder.' And when you have that happening, you've got a more combustible situation than you've ever had between the sexes."

If women are getting harder, their need for men is evaporating. Along with this, there is another great danger to men, of losing their strength to the woman, becoming softer, which can mean becoming impotent. For some men, being with women who are hard and competitive can be experienced as castration.

Dan believes that men are now rejecting the possibility of love in their lives as a backlash.

"I think more and more marriages are simply agreements, financial agreements. The modern way of looking at relationship is interesting, two people of opposite sexes both standing on their own two feet, with each owing the other nothing than their love—instead of one party being financially dependent upon the other. It's an interesting dream, but I don't think it's working. There's something about the roles between men and women—they've been developed for millions of years."

Roles between Men and Women

"When we become neuter gender something gets lost," Dan continued. "As women become less feminine they fall into the category of becoming more competitive. And women to-day think the men in their lives are all wimps. They are more convinced than ever before that men just really want sex from them. And if the men aren't able to feel good about themselves, and stand up to women, then it becomes true. And, men are less and less able to stand up to women these days. Do you notice the enormous proliferation of guys going with Asian women? Men are comfortable with women of other cultures because they don't perceive these women to be on the same fast track the guys are on."

Dan was asked if he thought a woman really wanted a strong man to stand up to her, declare boundaries. He said,

"I think that's the way it was classically set up. But now we have so few models left, so people's expectations of what you can get out of a marriage are gone. What about surrender and serving the other? *Nobody's strong enough to serve anymore, nobody's strong enough to surrender.* People see serving and surrender as weakness, but it's an enormous strength. They get caught in what I call power and control. When that happens marriage never reaches true intimacy. Love is not enough, one needs the whole structure for trust to grow."

Of course there are many men who are more concerned with love than money, men who value relationship and intimacy beyond all else. "What kind of guy would this be?" asked Dan. "I think he's basically a guy in trouble. If a man looks to the woman in his life to affirm him as a man, to affirm his masculinity, he's got a problem. A man must be affirmed by other men, or by himself, before he is able and ready to experience love with a woman."

Dan is speaking from the point of view of a man who has

a strong identification with his father. There are other men, however, who have felt primarily affirmed and loved by their mothers or other women in their lives. These men may not need the outer symbols of success in the male world that Dan speaks of. These men may turn to women as their natural source of validation and well-being. For these men, women are not frightening. It is competition with men that is more frightening to them.

Dan didn't always feel this way. He spent the earlier part of his life thinking differently.

"You know, I went until thirty-three being a creative writer, I didn't care much about money then, I wasn't so concerned about male or female roles. But things changed. I got married, and had a child. That hit me like a ton of bricks. What hit me was my daughter's eyes. I remember exactly the moment it happened. I rented a house out in Fire Island one summer, she was three. I was walking with her along a little boardwalk and she reached her hand up to touch a little flower blossom. Then she looked over at me and smiled. I said to myself—whew—her life is in my hands. I had a different understanding of what love meant them.

"I still have the poem I wrote that day. It's on a wall in my house, with a picture of my daughter from that summer, playing in the surf. The poem is about exactly this. That was the day I said, wait a minute, if I blow this one, I blow the big one. I had to find a business, a way to take care of her."

For Dan, making money, being able to take care of and provide for his family is his way of loving, of really being there. When he realized how needed he was by his daughter, this stirred the protector and provider in him. His concern with money is not for the sake of material gain alone, but so that

he can express his love and devotion in a way that is conso-
nant with his image of himself as a father and as a man.

I Love You Means I'll Do Things for You

"It's hard for a man to say I love you," Dan continued,
"because for a man to say I love you means I commit myself
to you. It means I'm going to start to do things for you, things
of a responsible nature to create this relationship and a life
together."

In order for Dan and men like him to love, they must feel
as though their home and relationship are a sanctuary, where
they are needed, valued, looked up to, and do not have to
compete for status, as they do at work. In order to be able to
be vulnerable to a woman, these men must feel as though they
are regarded highly, their self esteem must remain intact.
When this is in place, they will give of themselves fully to
the woman, and express it by being able to be counted on
completely, and providing for their needs. Women in relationships with men like Dan must understand that by working
hard and making a home for them, these men are saying I
love you. As Eric Fromm states, "Giving and loving are the
highest expression of potency. In the very act of giving, I
experience my strength, wealth, and power, my aliveness. In
the act of receiving, the woman gives."

Ultimately Women Have a Superior Position

Just the act of allowing himself to become vulnerable in a
relationship is a big step for most men. Alex, a medical student in his late twenties, feels that women today want too
much. He said,

"They want to work, succeed, have loads of money, and also want the man to love them. What they don't understand is that women inherently have a superior position because when a man falls in love with them, and becomes vulnerable, the man is deferring to them. He allows himself to be vulnerable, where he wouldn't necessarily otherwise. They have to leave him an arena where he can still claim his strength. If she is making as much money as he is, where can he feel in charge?

"Inherently the position of a woman is power, so, when you add to that women who want to be making more money than him, it crushes the man completely and doesn't leave any room for him to have something of his own. Some women want it both ways—they want to make big money and want the man to defer."

Vulnerability and openness to emotions is a sacrifice for some men. It makes them feel weaker, unable to maintain their usual defenses, at a disadvantage possibly. Women need to understand how to help a man feel strong when he loves, to enhance his dignity in every way. As men deal so much with competition in the workplace, it is painful for them to experience this in their love relationship as well.

The Hardest Thing about Love for a Man

When we look a little more broadly at what love means to a man, many don't speak about their relationships with their wives or girlfriends, which are conflicted, but with their relationships with their daughters, where they experience pure, unadulterated love.

"If you ask me what's the hardest and also the best thing in the world for a guy about love, it's what happens between him and his teenage daughter," said Jim, an Italian man. "Let me tell you, it can be heaven and it can be hell.

"Now I know a lot of guys, because of the various difference of ages in my children. I have friends who are just beginning to go through it with their teenage daughters. And these guys are captains of industries, I mean they've never known defeat in their life until their daughters become teenagers. These guys are really taken back by what happens. They really can't handle it. You try and tell them everyone goes through it, and it just proves that with all your worldly success, you're still human. They can't hear a word you say."

Clearly men's feelings for their daughters, and the importance that relationship plays in their lives, runs much deeper than they realize. Jim said it was hard to see her grow up and start dating.

"All of a sudden she's not Daddy's little girl anymore. This person has a mind of her own, and she's not just going to do what you say, because of who you are. Fathers go through a whole range of emotions then. They become despondent that they can't connect with their daughters anymore in the way they used to. It's a real, huge loss."

Dan, too, mentioned his love for his daughter in making crucial life changes. It seems that men allow themselves to love most freely—be most open and vulnerable with their daughters—because this is where they feel deeply needed and unconditionally loved. Their daughter's whole world depends upon them, at least for a while. They do not have to prove anything to her, but receive unconditional love and adoration just because they are there. This kind of relationship can be a safe haven from the outside world, and even from their marriages, where a man may have had to fight for and earn every bit of love and acknowledgment he receives from his wife.

"The worst moment comes," Jim continued, "when the daughters get their driver's licenses. This takes the tension to the highest level. It affects everything in a guy's life—his relationship with wife, his other children. Like in the show *The Sopranos*, there's this big mob leader and he is a hopeless pile of mush when it comes to his daughter, too. He can deal with major schemes much easier than he can deal with his daughter taking the car, because she's saying 'I'm in charge of my life. It's not you anymore.'

"I don't think most men are prepared for this. Until his daughter hits about ten or eleven, he doesn't believe that this wonderful, little angel is going to change. Once this break starts happening, the fathers questions everything, all his relationships. They wonder if they've been crazy, or duped. I've seen countless marriages suffer because of it. Sides are chosen. The mother will side with the daughter and he, the great provider, is cast aside. The fathers begin to feel like who they are is a meal ticket—just pay all the bills, take out the garbage, and don't say anything. The whole experience of fatherhood, that you're going to shelter and protect your daughter no matter what, that she can always come to you, is disappearing. You always want them to come back to Daddy for something."

This universal experience among men tells us a great deal about what it is a man needs to be able to love, what he wants. In his early relationship with his daughter the man is not scrutinized, judged, or compared to others. He is top of the mountain, just because he's there. She is innocent, accepting, and needs him completely. This provides the emotional security that allows him to give his heart completely, take care of her, and fully love.

> "When the daughters stop wanting that, you feel shunted aside," Jim continued. "The toughest part is when it first happens. By the time she walks down the aisle you're completely turned to mud, just glad you're invited to the wedding. You knew you were always going to have to pay for it, but for the last year or two you didn't know if you were getting an invitation."

In addition to learning about love from his daughter, Jim said,

> "Well, aside from my daughter, I learned most about love from a guy I worked for when I was a teenager at Sheinfelds Department Store. I was sixteen or seventeen and Syd Sheinfeld was thirty-three. He was a self-made guy who'd made a lot of money. To this very day, I try and lead my life by what he said to me every single day: 'What did you do to make the world a better place today?' Everyday I went to work, he said it. Even after I stopped working, and I went back to see him, and we talked over every subject known to man, I would try to act that way. Everyday I tried to do something good and make the world a better place. That's another way of looking at love.
>
> "Philosophically, Syd Sheinfeld's my hero. He had to quit college early and go to work because his father died, so he did things later on in life. He studied music and taught at the synagogue. He told me one time he went into the synagogue to teach the kids. The way he did it was to call them anti-Semitic names. Then he'd tell them, 'See, this is what

life is like. Get used to it. Don't let people who use this language stop you from doing what you want to do. Never let them stop you from feeling love. Just realize that people who attack like that are frightened. Don't panic, just realize this person has a weakness and there's nothing wrong with you. Be good to everyone, and your life will really be something.'

"As far as I'm concerned," Jim continued, "Syd Sheinfeld really knew what it mean to love."

A Broader View of Love

When we take a broader view of love, we see the importance of stopping personal self-absorption and being willing to give to others. We are then touching upon one of the simple laws of love.

Ernie Castaldo, singer, performer in the original *West Side Story*, vocal coach, handsome, in his fifties, teaches the Sedona Releasing Method, which is about releasing stress and other negativities in order to be available to love.

"As a teacher of the Sedona Method I've worked with many individuals and couples, and of course all anybody ever really wants is love. They may call it many things, but deep down, we're all hungering for love.

"It can be hard for men and women in relationships to have an ongoing experience of love because men tend to be more logical and women more in touch with their feelings. Women offer men another point of view. Men have to be able to accept that. If men could get in tune with where the woman is, their communication would be much better. Ultimately, to me, real communication is love.

"For love to happen both have to get quiet, really take a

moment, and realize that they don't always hear what the other person is saying by the words. I was talking to a friend the other day, he was saying things to me, and nothing added up. I said, 'I hear your words, but what are you saying?' He said, 'Well, it's hard.' I replied, 'You're telling me it feels hard to you. Now I know what you're saying.'

A lot of times we may dismiss the other person, because they're not where we are at. Just take time to find out what they're really trying to say."

The feelings of love between two individuals create an environment in which communication can flow. This environment consists of openness, acceptance and the willingness to really hear. If communication is blocked, or flagging, the experience of being loved will also feel absent. Some may say that to be understood is to be loved.

Take Time to Connect

"The wonderful thing about love," Ernie said, "is that when you're with someone you love very much, you don't have to say anything. Sometimes you even feel as though you know what they're thinking and what they need, before they say it."

When two people are in tune, it can sometimes be easy to know what is needed and wanted. It is always dangerous, however, to assume we definitely know what the other is thinking, as projection can easily come into play. What Ernie is talking about here is the willingness to be sensitive to the other's feelings, to anticipate what they might want, and be willing to give it. It is also always wise to take a moment and ask if this is what they truly want, or are thinking of.

"It's a busy world, but we've got to make time to be together," Ernie said. "A man should be able to say that he
needs time and understanding. Most men have trouble doing
that. They also have a hard time admitting they've ever been
wrong. Ego gets in the way of love. Each party has to take
responsibility for honoring the other's position, and seeing if
they can adjust to it. Once a woman knows the man cares,
she'll often be willing to do much to make him happy."

Ernie is pointing to the crucial importance of being willing
to put aside not only time, but one's own personal point of
view, to enter the world of the other, in order to understand
more deeply what they are feeling and truly need from you.
In this manner, love becomes a teacher that helps us to tran-
scend our tunnel vision and grow. It also helps us to find inner
resources we may not have known we had, so that we can
provide the other with that which he or she is asking for.

Feeling Needed

There are different factors which bring two people together, and also which permit the relationship to last.

"In the beginning," said Ernie, "I think it is need that brings
people together. Then at a certain point, you get to a level
where you are complete. If the relationship is working, it has
helped you become complete in yourself. So, after awhile
need can be an obstacle After awhile you're both standing
on your own two feet."

There is an enormous difference between need and love.
When two people need one another to feel whole, they are
focused upon their deficiencies, what they are getting to fill

up the gap. When two people love one another, they are focused upon what they can give one another, out of the fullness of who they are.

> "At one point when my mother was ill," Ernie continued, "I had to stop some of my activities to care for her. I thought I wouldn't be able to live without those activities, but I learned that I can live under all situations. I don't have to cling. We think we're dependent on so many things, but things change in life. If you have yourself, you survive everything and are more able to love."

Love Versus Attachment

What Ernie is speaking about here is the difference between love and attachment. For many people being attached to another, being possessive, dependent, or in need is thought to be love. When they no longer feel that way, they think their love has died. They have not read the wonderful poem of Kabir that states, "An emotion that is here one moment and gone the next cannot be called love."

Love must be differentiated from passing feelings, or states of mind. Real love grows in many ways, ways which include service, deeds of love, sacrifice, surrender, true communication, and the ability to be still and listen—the ability to give up preconceived thoughts and plans.

> "I know marriages where people have not strayed," Ernie said. "The simple answer is they never felt the need. And people who did stray, at the time felt the need. It could have come from wanting more experiences, or feeling that a different person gave them a sense of safety or adventure. I think, realistically, each person goes into marriage with cer-

tain values and intentions, and they sometimes change, and that's part of what we're dealing with."

Needless to say, the ability to deal with change is a crucial ingredient in love. Sometimes people will withhold love because their partner or situation has changed. But love teaches us how to weather change, accept fluctuation, and be willing to let go of using the relationship as a safe haven against life. This is the same as the practice of forgiveness, which is the ability to let go of what has happened, release judgment and be available for the person and situation now. One might say that acceptance of the person, as they evolve, is the very essence of love.

"We give a guarantee, I'm with you forever and ever," Ernie said, "but agreements are broken all the time. That's always a possibility. Sometimes you've gotten what you need from a partner and they move on, or you do. Moving on doesn't have to mean the end of love. We just love differently then, that's all."

For many people, when a marriage or other relationship is over, much bitterness remains behind. But the love they shared over the years can still remain alive if they have been able to acknowledge the goodness that was present, the many gifts they received, and now give the partner the gift of going forward to something else they need now.

When we let a person go with love, rather than bitterness or anger, the love we send out to them returns to us in many ways, especially in our ability to go forward in our own lives.

"All of this must be spoken of openly," Ernie continued. "If one person is feeling attracted to someone else it shouldn't be hidden, but shared. To me love is having the freedom to talk about it to their partner and not being afraid of consequences. Talking about it might defuse it. Thought and feelings precede action. If the thought and feelings are expressed, they don't have to build and grow into action. It can just be a thought or feeling and sometimes it subsides."

Listening *and* Hearing

Especially when confronting change, the ability to really listen to the other and take in what they are saying, can be equated with love.

"When a man is communicating the woman needs to listen without getting emotional," Ernie said. "Many men won't communicate with their wives because she gets too emotional and they can't stand it. So, being willing to listen, not putting your own needs in the way of another's communication, is loving. I think love is sacrifice. To really hear the other you have to sacrifice where you're at, hear what they're saying, and try to give them what they're asking for."

This kind of sacrifice, (also called surrender of ego), brings the highest returns. It opens the door for real union with another, also called communion.

To Love Someone Is to Take Them Out of a Box

"Most of the time we put a person into a box called husband or wife," Ernie said, "and they stay stuck there. To love someone is to take them out of any box you've put them in. A box can turn into a coffin, and love becomes buried and

withers away. Love is sacrificing your need to confine them
Love is letting someone be who they are.

"There are some marriages that don't last because the
partners grow so differently. And what's wrong with that?
Nothing. Love is all inclusive, not all exclusive. We try to
make it fit into a little picture of how love is supposed to be.
It doesn't work that way, and we know it. You can't tell the
heart who to love. Some of us only fall in love with the most
unlikely candidates. It doesn't make sense, but there it is. As
soon as you start controlling someone, it's like crushing them
in your hand.

"In the Sedona Method, one of our teachers, Virginia
Lloyd always said, 'Love is wanting for the other what they
want for themselves, even if you aren't the one able to give
it to them.' "

Ernie is coming from the highest peak of understanding of
love, which is the ability to know, accept and give to the other
without judgment or selfishness. From this standpoint we realize that love is giving, and that what is good for the other,
is good for us as well. This point of view about love separates
it from selfish grasping, or making the other an object to fulfill
our own needs. Although it takes time to grow into this way
of living, we all have experiences of it, and if we decide to,
can choose to make this way of love a part of our daily routine. Ultimately, nothing is more satisfying.

Nothing but Love

Thom Lisk, head of the Thom Lisk Speaker's Bureau, is
happy to say, that for him there is nothing but love in his
relationship with his second wife.

"I have learned so much about love," he says, "and keep learning more every day. In fact, I've just taken out an ad in the newspaper to wish my wife a happy anniversary. It's been nine years and I'm more in love with her now than when we first married. That is because both of us have a strong commitment to love."

Thom is an example of a man who has made a commitment to learning from the mistakes in his first marriage, and making sure they don't happen again.

"If I'm not conscious of my weaknesses and tendencies, I could repeat in my second marriage the same mistakes I made in my first," he said. "In fact, if I knew then what I know now, I could have loved my first wife better. Men need to take responsibility for their loving in their relationships."

This is a unique and profound statement of his absolute willingness to take responsibility for his own contribution to the marriage, and for his own former errors. Rather than constantly watch and count what is being given, Thom is willing to be the one to give first.

"I believe you must give first, if you want to receive," he said. "I give her hugs whenever I see her, to let her know I care. Men need a lot of touching and hugging as well, not necessarily sex, but affection, and most are embarrassed to acknowledge this. But men can get isolated and lonely, especially after a long day in business. When a man comes home the physical contact with his wife is important and feels good. Research has shown that men need twelve hugs a day. I believe many men start extramarital affairs not so much because of their sexual needs as their needs for affection, warmth and human contact."

In order to keep love growing, all needs must be addressed, including the simple need for affection, touching, intimacy, and letting a man know it matters to the woman that he's there.

"All men really need to know how to love a woman," Thom Lisk continued. "Before I can become intimate with my wife, I need to give her quality time, listen to her, ask good questions and get her to speak to me. I must establish an atmosphere of closeness, where everything naturally follows.

"It is enormously important to many women to have this feeling of being cared for and loved before having physical intimacy. For some men, this is seen as an annoyance. However, when there is a commitment to love, not just to pleasure, the time is well worth taking, and enhances the entire experience ultimately."

Mr. Lisk views his marriage as a sacrament, a place to deepen his love for his wife, and also for God.

"By serving her, I am serving God," he says. "When God is a partner in your relationship, there is no end to the love available. In fact, there is a quote from the New Testament which speaks of it this way: 'A man is to lay down his life for his wife, just as Jesus laid down his life for his wife, the church.' "

Mr. Lisk's religious orientation lifts his relationship to another level. The love that is generated and maintained between him and his wife is simultaneously given to the world and to

God. This frame of reference is an enormous assistance for him in understanding the purpose of his relationship and in fulfilling it.

Ultimately, we must all think about the source of love, where it comes from, what allows it to flow. When we maintain close contact with this source, our lives are refreshed daily, like an ever flowing stream. When anger, resentment or other experiences block the flow, our lives become constricted and lonely. In a very real sense, it is wise to let go of constrictions and let the love flow again. This is the best medicine, not only for ourselves, but the entire world.

Touchstones to Remember

1. We are all love. We must learn to realize and acknowledge this.

2. A man must realize he is not his money. Whether he has a lot or little, he is fully deserving of love.

3. If a man isn't able to feel good about himself and his masculinity, he may find it hard to love.

4. Serving and surrender are not weakness, but take enormous strength.

5. Saying "I Love You" means commitment to men. It means, "I'm going to do things for you."

6. Men and women bond differently. Each may have different needs for intimate time together. Learn about and respect the differences. Love can be expressed in many ways.

7. Men love to shelter and protect their daughters, who give them unconditional love. The more a man feels

unconditionally loved and regarded, the easier it is for him to love.

8. True communication is love. Take time to get in tune with the other person. Give the gift of listening, hearing, and giving what is asked for.

9. Love is not attachment, possession, dependency or control. Real love is knowing and honoring the other, just as they are.

10. When a man feels safe and cared for, he usually stays in a relationship and allows the bond to deepen.

SEVEN

Men and Sex

A man's sense of himself is heavily influenced by his sexual prowess, anatomy, and attractiveness. Some men must have endless conquests to prove that they are of value, that beautiful women desire them. Some need to parade these women around on their arms to show the world their trophies, how spectacular both they and the women are. This is sexuality as narcissism, ego, falling in love with a reflection of yourself and using the other person to build up a false sense of value and of self.

Some men must beat out other men in obtaining the prize. They long to steal women away, not for the joy of having her, but for the thrill of showing that he can win—is "the best man." This is sexuality as war. The woman is an object to conquer—other men are vanquished. In this way some men prove that they are as good as or better than their fathers, the original competitors. Once these men actually have a woman, they may not have any idea of what to do with her, nor may they really want her. It's then onto another, for the thrill of winning again.

Sexuality expresses many aspects of a man's psyche: love, hate, revenge, play, rebellion, work and duty. It has different roles in a man's life at different times. For some men it turns into addiction, a way of controlling other aspects of their world, or avoiding other issues.

Personal Inventory: Men And Sex

Group A: Warriors, Heroes, Adventurers
Group B: Lovers, Dreamers, Peter Pans
Group C: Controllers, Perfectionists, Addicts
Group D: Wise Men, Gurus, Seers
Group E: A Real Guy!

SCORING
(Score each question from 1–4 in the following manner)

1. Not at all
2. Sometimes
3. Often
4. All the time

1. Are many sexual conquests important to him?

2. Is sex a game with him?

3. How important is it to him to be seen as a good lover?

4. Does sex serve as a form of relaxation or reduction of tension?

5. Do sex and emotional intimacy go together for him? After sex, does he like to stay around?

6. How important is sex in his life? Is it something he enjoys?

7. How much pressure does he feel to perform well in sex?

8. Can he love and have sex with the same woman?

9. Is sex seen as a cosmic experience?

10. Does he have special rituals and tastes without which he cannot have sex?

11. Is romance as important as sex to him? Does one without the other work?

12. Must he have constant new experiences in sex? Does he get bored easily?

13. Does it spoil the sexual experience if it is filled with responsibility?

14. Is sex natural and easy for him? Free of guilt?

15. Does he feel sex is only for marriage?

16. Is he loyal, and monogamous because that's just what feels right?

17. Does he rate his sexual performance and that of his partner each time he has sex?

18. Is sex a spontaneous expression of warmth, enjoyment and caring?

19. Does he have to engage in secret sex without the knowledge of his partner?

20. Does sex feel unnecessary for him because he is so fulfilled by love?

ANSWERS

Group A: Warriors, Heroes, Adventurers
(Questions 1, 2, 4, 12) Score 12 or more

These men see sex as another place to achieve conquests. Not only do they require variety and challenge, but often become bored if there is not variety in the experience. These men often want external stimulants as well, to make them feel as though they are on the cutting edge.

Group B: Lovers, Dreamers, Peter Pans
(Questions 3, 6, 11, 13) Score 12 or more

This man's identity is caught up with being a good lover. His sexual experience and needs are often tied up with a great deal of romance. He enjoys nights alone together and times walking at the sea. Sex is infused with poetry for him, and often, being tied down or having other responsibilities to the partner can spoil it.

Group C: Controllers, Perfectionists, Addicts
(Questions 7, 10, 17, 19) Score 12 or more

Many of these men use sex for control, or to establish their dominance over their partner. They judge themselves and others for their performance and demand that their special needs and tastes be met. They also tend to be suspicious and possessive of their partners, fearing that they are trying to find someone else and undermine their control.

Group D: Wise Men, Gurus, Seers
(Questions 5, 9, 15, 20) Score 12 or more

These men see sex as a transcendental experience, connecting them to the divine. For some it is heavily regulated by prohibitions. When sex is permitted it is not just sex, but love making, a form of deep communion, uniting the two souls. Some reject sex completely, feeling it is a lower or impure way of expressing the great love and oneness they feel.

Group E: A Real Guy!
(Questions 8, 14, 16, 18) Score 12 or more

Sex is a natural, enjoyable expression of warmth, closeness and often love between two partners. These individuals are able to feel good about themselves and their partners, and be flexible about their sexual expression. Sometimes it is connected to love, other times it can be just good fun.

Men Have a Need for Sex—Woman Have a Need for Love

Anthony, a handsome, single attorney in his mid-forties has been with many women. Although he says he wants to settle down, no woman fits the bill.

"One of the things that men have a problem with," Anthony said, "is telling a woman exactly how he feels about her, in bed and out. The women don't want to hear what men really have to tell them. They think as long as they give you good sex nothing else should matter. This is a major issue because men fear the women can't handle the real experience they're having."

Anthony is suggesting that men don't share what really goes on for them sexually with women. They may feel a woman can't handle the truth here, that she is making sex out to be more than it is for him.

> "Let's face it, a lot of the time, a woman is more in love with the man than the man is in love with her. Lots of women turn sex into love. Men don't. For a man sex is fine just the way it is. Sometimes there's love there too, but most of the time there isn't. Men have a need for sex. Women have a need for love. This creates problems. I'm not saying men don't have a need for love too, but for them, sex and love can be very different. This creates problems for men. It does for me. I can't stand being with a woman who says how much she loves me when all I want is good sex. It makes me feel lousy about myself."

In a case like this the man must split himself and live a lie. He shuts out what the woman is saying because he can't reciprocate or tell her what is true for him. This lie can go on for just so long. It finally causes him to take off one day—with everyone feeling the worse for it, and the woman not understanding what happened.

Being Faithful in Body and Mind

> "There are other problems too," Anthony continued. "Often a man feels he can't be faithful to a woman, but how can he say that? How can he even tell her that a lot of the time in bed, he's unfaithful in his mind. He can't tell her who he's making love with in his mind while he's making love with her. And believe me, a lot of the time he's making love with one woman in his mind, while he's physically in bed

with someone else. This kind of thing happens to lots of guys. Sometimes when they're in bed with one woman, they suddenly start thinking of someone else, someone they might not even realize they were wanting. Maybe you've seen some woman on television or in a film and it's created a sensual desire for her. Well, she'll come to you when you're making love. Then how do you think a guy feels if the woman he's physically in bed with starts telling him how much she loves him?"

Anthony has a strong conscience and sense of integrity which causes him pain when he feels he is lying or betraying another, even in his mind. Deep within he longs for straight-forwardness and honesty though he feels it is not possible.

"Sometimes a man does love a woman and is afraid of losing her. He knows she wants to feel like she is the only one. Most guys can't give her that. I know I can't. I don't think men are wired up to want only one person their entire lives. That's why they have a real problem with honesty and sex-uality. It's built on a fairytale world that just isn't so."

Anthony and men like him compensate for the lack of ability to be honest about sex, with dishonesty.

"I see men lying all the time, telling her she's the only one, or saying they feel a lot more for her than they actually do. Getting steady sex from a woman can be a pretty strong inducement to say lots of things, especially since women seem to need to build sex up to be more than it is. They need to turn it into love, and believe that the man will always love them."

It is important for women to understand this fundamental mechanism in the male psyche—that sex does not necessarily mean love to a man, and that good sex is no assurance that the relationship will go any further.

"Sometimes the woman wants to get married and he doesn't want to marry her," Anthony continued. "He may like the relationship the way it is. He may not even know what the woman's goals are in the relationship and he doesn't want to find out. Or, he may really love her but she doesn't satisfy his fantasy. Having a woman you love and want to be with, but who doesn't fulfill your sexual fantasy can be a big problem. In a case like that the man will want both the woman he loves and also another, to fulfill his sexual fantasy. A man, in bed, needs a woman who satisfies his fantasy more than he needs a woman he loves. Remember sex is sex, and love is love. Even though it sounds, rotten, I'm telling it like it is. But there's no rules. Not anymore."

No Rules

The fact that relationships, including sexual relationships, are no longer governed by traditional expectations and role models allows all kinds of behavior and the psychological stress that arises from it to be prevalent. The availability of sex for Anthony, and many men like him, makes commitment, marriage, and even love, less urgent. It also creates a situation where lying, games and lack of integrity can become an everyday experience, causing another kind of pain.

Whore-Madonna Complex

Anthony is a good example of many men who feel split between sexuality and love. There are women who are good for having sex with, and there are the women you love. In the extreme, this condition has been called the Whore-Madonna Complex, in which a man splits his perception into the good woman, (Madonna, Mother) and the bad woman, (the Whore). The good woman becomes the wife and mother of his children, the bad woman, becomes the one he allows himself to have sexual fantasies with and physically enjoy. In some cases this complex is so severe that men can't sleep with their wives much, or if they do, they receive little satisfaction. These men see sex as dirty or bad, not something to be done with good women. The problem has nothing to do with their wives, but with the way in which they perceive their own sexuality and the fantasies that accompany it. When there is a split between the good and bad woman like this, it is almost impossible to experience love, commitment and sexual satisfaction in the same place at the same time.

Getting Sex Wherever He Can

Unlike Anthony, Frank, a good-looking mechanic in his late twenties, feels no compunction about getting and enjoying sex whenever he can. Raised in a generation where sex was available without repercussions, he enjoyed speaking about his sex life.

"It's a game," he said. "I like to get it whenever I can. If someone seems to be interested in me, I'll tell them you're a beautiful person. Pretty soon after that, I'll start telling them I love them. Why not? It makes them feel good. We sleep together. I feel good. Everybody wins. I guess I do love them for that time. It doesn't mean I'll love them forever. I've done that with a lot of women. I'll do it if I think I can get something from them, sexual favors usually. If you tell women you love them, they're hooked. Even if they're not really attractive, I do it. Why not? Anyone can become attractive if she feels loved. I've seen it happen under my eyes. Maybe it's not fair or kind, because in truth I really wouldn't be interested in them except for what I can get at the moment. But I believe women get something from this too. We all need good experiences. So I'll give them compliments and approval all night long."

All night long doesn't translate into all year long for Frank. He takes what he gets and moves on.

Playing Love Games

Frank feels conflicted about living this way,

"Sometimes I feel a little bit like a thief, ripping them off, because I wasn't telling the whole truth, but that only lasts a minute. I also wonder if they're telling the truth to me? Probably not. You just take that for granted. I think everyone lies and you can't trust anyone. It's not really lies, we're just playing love games. That's what life is. You say I'll be this—and you'll be that—I'll tell you this and you'll tell me that. You don't really expect much more these days."

Frank does wish for honesty in his relationships. He said, "Sometimes I wish we could all take one day a year and tell the truth about how we really feel. What a day that would be. On that day you would not be worried about wondering how am I scoring—how do I look?"

There's a disconnection between Frank's short-term impulses and emotions and his long-range sense of life. Right now he seems to have nothing other than short-term gratification in mind. The future spreads out as a blanket of encounters he gets out of fast. He uses his charm to get what he can. Some might label him sociopathic, or a con man, using others as objects and lacking a sense of guilt or shame. He can also be seen as a product of a society where everything goes, where there is plentiful sex and few consequences. However, there are emotional consequences for Frank, though he may not be aware of them. After the immediate gratification subsides, he is left without faith or trust in himself, or anyone. For him, a relationship is just getting and giving momentary pleasure. Underneath his surface charm, lies a deep distrust of others, and of love.

If Frank had his day of truth with a woman he would say,

"I love you. I'm happy you're here with me. I want you to stay, I don't want to go away. But I don't want heartache and trouble. The truth is I do love people and that's how I feel. I wish I could just smile at everyone and say, hey, I really care about you. If I actually did that, of course everyone would think I was nuts. It's okay to do it for a little while with women though, before sex. So I do."

There is a refreshing quality to Frank's open confession of his desire for basic love and connection. In an almost childlike manner he channels this fundamental human need into his casual, sexual relationships which don't turn into "trouble" for him. For men as well as women, sexual contact can bring a temporary sense of freedom from separation, loneliness, and feelings of failure in life.

Hungry for Sex

Despite their needs and hungers, not all men are able to act out their sexuality in the way described above.

"One thing that amazed me is that sexually, so many people have never become fulfilled," Mr. Pankau said. "I hear this over and over in my work. They're hungry for sex. And it's not only the men. I dated a woman who was forty years old and she never had an orgasm in her life with her husband. He never put much into the relationship and she never got fulfilled. I find this is very common.

"I think the reason for this is that many men are ashamed to say to their partner that they're unfulfilled, or be able to hear that from the woman. The people I talk to say, 'We've been married for four years—we have sex, it takes ten minutes.' I say, if you don't have an hour, well what can you expect? Most people don't realize that. It takes time to make sex good and important."

Hunger to be Touched

"I was talking to someone the other day," Ed continued, "and he said no woman had ever massaged him or rubbed his back, or anything like that. He never got that kind of intimacy. He must feel so lonely in his body. There's a body hunger to be touched, I believe. The same thing emotionally. A guy needs to hear 'You're wonderful in bed, you make me happy. I think you're great.' "

Mr. Pankau believes this behavior is universal.

"I work with men from all over. Most of them have never taken the time to learn how to have an emotional relationship. Partly because it's not manly. Partly, they never saw this intimate relationship at home so they don't know how to do it. They see it in movies, but how many people have a life like they see in the movies? So, they go on the Internet looking for something they can't find at home. The reason men go to the Internet is that they can't establish something in person, so they can on a fantasy level. It's safe for lots of married men too, because they have the illusion of having intimacy, even though they don't want to take it to the next step in real life."

Most men and women automatically repeat the patterns they grew up with at home, and live out the unconscious assumptions they made about relationships. It takes effort, work, time and the willingness to step back and look at your life, to redefine how you want your relationships to be now.

No Intention of Stopping Being Unfaithful

Arnold, an upstanding, attractive man in his early fifties, is the rotary club president, and views himself as a real pillar of society who stands for good values. Despite his public persona he said,

"I've been unfaithful to my wife on an ongoing basis for most of my marriage. And I have no intention of stopping now. We've been married for twenty-three years, have three children, and there's nothing bad about my wife except that she's a cold fish in bed. Everything else works, the house, house cleaning, bringing up the kids, great. But in bed, it's nowhere. We have sex once in awhile because it's time to have it. But there's no affection and warmth. So, I fool around. I'm afraid to tell her because I don't know what would happen. I don't want to lose my property or children. Telling her would mess things up."

In a sense Arnold feels justified in his behavior because of his wife's ungivingness in bed. He's a man who can't live with so little sex, and yet who wants to keep his marriage intact.

"Yeah, I feel guilty all the time," Arnold said. "I mess around with different people. Right now I have a beautiful young women. When it started I said, 'Look I'm married, but if you'd like to we can have a few drinks.' So this particular relationship has been going on for about three years now. She's terrific. She has a body to die for, and she loves sex. I feel younger, happier, I can let out my energy. I'm even much nicer to my wife."

For some men, an extramarital affair improves their marriages, even allows it to keep going on. They receive their sexual gratification with their lovers, and the stability of a home life with their wives. Underneath this, however, is often anger and sometimes revenge with the wife.

Arnold said,

"I feel okay about doing this because my wife's attitude is, well it's our anniversary, so we'll have sex, or, it's your birthday. She trades things for sex—if you come with me to my parents, then when we get home, I'll take care of you. Very degrading. I'm a physical person, a sensual person. I want both of us to enjoy. Because sex is a problem for us, is that a reason to break up a marriage, to ruin an entire family?"

Arnold doesn't see the sexual problem between himself and his wife as an expression of deeper issues between them, of an unwillingness on the part of his wife to give to him. He also doesn't see how rejected and hurt he feels and how he works this out by having other women, maybe in part, to get back at her too.

Going through the Motions

Arnold said,

"I can't tell her what I'm doing because it would break her heart. Sometimes I'm afraid she's going to find out, because sometimes I secretly want to be punished, or I want to punish her. I want to say look what you've done. We have three children and maybe we had sex five times. I feel like I have no choice about what I'm doing. This is making me into someone I don't like."

Arnold has a sense of how this kind of behavior corrodes his self-worth and self-respect. Although he receives sexual satisfaction he pays the price with the loss of his integrity. For a man who lives as a pillar of the community, this secret sexual life takes a toll.

Arnold feels he may be addicted to sex. He said,

"Well, if time goes by and I don't have it, I get nervous. The woman I'm with now gives me all I need and that keeps me comfortable. Recently, though, she has asked me several times what would the future would hold for us? She knows I'm not happy at home. She's young, attractive, and has lots going for her. There's more than sex between us, there's genuine affection. I worry about her too. This kind of life doesn't give her what she needs. She deserves more than this and I recognize that. How long can this go on?"

Arnold recognizes that his affairs can go nowhere. Sooner or later he must deal with the loss of a partner, in this case someone he likes, values and admires. He also regrets his limitations in providing his partners with what they fully need and want in their lives. There are many areas of frustration and disturbance. Although this arrangement may fulfill some temporary needs, it cannot go on forever.

"When I go home there's a space that's not filled," Arnold continued. "But I keep wondering if it is worth leaving just for sex? The kids are growing up. Soon they'll all be gone. They won't be too proud of their old man if I do leave, but I hope they'll understand. I don't relish the rest of my life with these lies and with the coldness. It's not a rosy path I see. The wife's more like a friend or social director. She seems to be sublimating whatever sexual desire she feels. Sometimes I wonder if she doesn't know about my affairs, and that this arrangement might not suit her just fine? My time is not all accounted for and she never says anything."

There are many marriages in which there are unspoken, perhaps unconscious agreements between the partners to allow one or the other to fulfill their sexual desires elsewhere, thereby taking strain off the marriage, and allowing it to continue. Without this kind of outlet, the man would never remain. Some wives may even be unconsciously grateful for the "other woman" who keeps her home safe and secure.

"What I want to say to my wife," Arnold continued, "is, what are you holding on to? Just because your mother was like that with your father doesn't mean you have to be that way. What makes you so tight and uptight? It's not like you can't have sex—but you won't. But you don't realize what it's doing to me. So, if you make your bed, sweetheart, you'll lie in it—maybe, one day, alone."

Arnold tacitly realizes that this arrangement with his wife too, cannot go on permanently. Once the task of child rearing is over, many men leave long-term relationships in order to find the gratification they couldn't get with their wives. Families are vulnerable when the kids leave the nest, and if these issues aren't addressed openly and worked at long before that moment comes, divorce is often inevitable. Honest communication, and mutual giving and taking, go a long way to preventing the marriage breaking up.

Gay Sexuality

Gay sexuality is a complicated matter. There are many factors which cause a man to choose a same sex partner as their primary relationship. The stereotype that gay men have rejected their fathers and identified with their mothers is simplistic. There are many gay men who feel strong in their masculinity, and have fine relationships with their fathers, and with their mothers as well.

Howard Rossen is a therapist for gay and straight men.

"I do a lot of work with sexuality," he says, "which has a very powerful impact on everybody. I think straight men and gay men are very much affected by their sexual instincts. It encompasses all of their functioning. The whole oedipal connection, the boys longing for the mother and fear of the father, affects every man. It affects men in different ways though. Some men long for the father, and want to be like the mother. Some men appreciate the woman's sensitivity, honor and identify with it. They do not identify with their fathers.

"Once you cross that boundary into gay functioning, all the usual structures of sexual expression are torn down, so you have to put your own structure in. That's what makes gay relationships difficult."

The freedom a man feels to express himself in anyway he chooses, also creates a great deal of fluidity in gay relationships. There can be a constant desire for new forms of expression and experimentation, which includes new partners. The benefits gained in greater self-expression are balanced by the lack of stability in many of these relationships.

"In the gay world sexuality is rampant, you can express it any way. Fidelity is tougher, because in the gay world it's acceptable not to be faithful. And you can be anonymous and have lots of casual sexual experiences. In the heterosexual world it's culturally appropriate to be monogamous, so it's harder to break that. People are caught by the worlds and norms they choose to live in."

For some, part of the lure of being gay is the freedom from commitment and the ability to experiment in a culturally accepted way. For some, the burden of raising a family, and being in a conventional lifestyle is suffocating. For others, there is no sense of having any choice at all in this matter. If they did have choice, they would choose a heterosexual lifestyle, due to the difficulties a gay lifestyle presents.

"Emotional commitment is hard for gay men," Howard Rossen said. "For gay men you're dealing with rejection, by others and the self—deep, deep rejection of who you really are. You're dealing with deep, negative images about being gay, that have been planted in your being. I'm talking about internalized homophobia. I see it in my practice all the time. When you realize from the day you were five years old that you liked that little boy, and you wanted to play with a doll, you were told 'No, that's wrong.' Somebody negated your feelings and you realized I'd better keep quiet and hide this. You go into the closet as a little child. It becomes your defensive tool. You never let go of it. You pretend to be somebody you're not. This is deep internalized feeling that you're a bad guy. How can a bad guy live the truth, or emotionally commit to another person?"

The biggest struggle many gay men have is with identity, being able to know, acknowledge and accept who they are, being able to give themselves something society hasn't—validation—not only of their sexuality, but of all aspects of their lives. Until a man comes to peace with who he is, and truly likes himself, real satisfaction is impossible.

"The gay man has had a lot of damage in his experiences about what it is to love," said Howard Rossen. "You often experience rejection from a parent, because you're gay. On some level a parent is fearful of it, and without planning to, a father pulls back. It may not be overt, but God knows it is tremendously damaging. Fathers are so uncomfortable about having gay sons that they withdraw. Love becomes diminished, even if it's not a conscious choice. They don't know how to deal with it so they withdraw and the mother fills the void. You get a strong mother-son bond. That's always damaging because the twinship relationship between father and son is crucial. A father needs to be an icon."

A great deal of the pain a gay man may suffer is not necessarily from his sexuality, but from the rejection of his parents, from the loss of their love. He then defines himself as an outcast, and this inner definition can become cast in stone. In all dimensions of his life, not only his sexuality, he then may feel like an outcast with no way of being redeemed.

"As a therapist, I work with gay men and find a way of ameliorating that deep, internalized sense of homophobia, of self-hate," Mr. Rossen said. "We work to reach a greater level of self-respect. As that happens, their ability to accept relationships that have both sex and love grows."

To Be Vulnerable Is Incredibly Masculine

There are qualities gay men have or are able to express, that straight men lack, or have to hide, according to Mr. Rossen.

"To be vulnerable is incredibly masculine, but in our culture it is not. We don't look at vulnerability as a masculine trait; it's a feminine trait. The straight man has an incredible fear of being sensitive, being vulnerable to the woman. Many are so involved with being macho, with being a man in a power position, they don't realize the sensitivity you need in a relationship is absent. The male macho pose gets in their way. Heterosexual men cannot express vulnerability, they have to repress it. They sublimate all their vulnerability into aggressive energy.

"Straight men often don't realize that women love and want to see the man's flaws and be there for him. A woman can take that vulnerability and work with it, it can be rich in a relationship. I think gay men understand this better. They allow much more vulnerability with each other. With gay men there is a greater connection to the feminine, intuitive side, the anima."

Because gay men are freer to play multiple roles, it is easier for many of them to get in touch with others aspects of their beings, such as their vulnerability.

Role Playing

"When a man acknowledges that he is gay, he becomes free of many things. For instance, gay sex seems to be freer, especially when it comes to role playing. You play feminine, masculine, passive, aggressive, it's part of the sexual game. However, if one is into role playing on every level of relationship, there's trouble. Something is always missing then. If you only play the passive role you're missing something, strength and dominance. If you just play the strong dominant role, you miss the vulnerability. Socially, we do this too. We go into our social life as if we're playing a part. The man who has lots of sex is considered a stud. The woman who has lots of sex is a slut. There's no complimentary word in our entire lexicon for a woman who is sexual. She's looked down upon. An older man and a younger woman is considered to be fine. If a woman goes out with a younger guy, she's a dirty old lady. There's something impure about sexuality for a woman. These are all the roles we get plugged into."

Sexuality can be viewed in the context of role playing, as the need and ability to play a variety of roles. Many long-lasting relationships are those which allow this kind of freedom, within the boundaries of the relationship itself.

"I've had a lot of gay men who've gotten married, and then they realized, what am I doing? I have a patient right now, very successful in his profession, well-known, married, with a son who he adores. He and his wife have not had sexual relations in about a year. He's realizing it's a sham. He didn't realize he was gay before he married her. He was attracted to men, but kept trying to make it go away. Now he's realizing what's going on."

Many men cannot tolerate living a gay lifestyle. They long for the acceptance and stability a heterosexual marriage provides, and will try to suppress homosexual desires in the effort to keep a heterosexual lifestyle going, (or will have occasional, secret homosexual affairs). Some can do this their entire lives, others reach a breaking point.

"It's hard for this patient to leave," Mr. Rossen continues, "because it's socially acceptable to be with a woman and our entire society is designed to support that. His greatest fear is the effect of this on his son. I think he just needs to be a good father and trust that, as he explores his own sexuality. I am not convinced that he can't give his son a good role model and explore his sexuality. I am encouraging him to be honest with his feelings, which are getting in the way of his living. I asked him how he would feel when his son was twenty, and he was out on his own, about fifty or sixty, but had continued all these years in a totally unsatisfying relationship?"

There are many points of view regarding this crucial question. From Howard Rossen's point of view, in order for a man to live with full mental and emotional health, he must live in a way that is true to himself. Beyond the lack of sexual satisfaction it is living a lie that is most damaging, pretending to be someone you are not, living with lack of self acceptance which often grows into self-hate.

I Am Fragile, I Am Vulnerable

"What a gay man, (and probably also many straight men) can't say and needs to tell you is, 'I am fragile, I am vulnerable, I am a product of my family and all issues I've experienced growing up. I put on a brave, macho, strong, social, masculine face, but I am a fragile entity, just as everybody else. Be gentle with me. I need to nurture and be nurtured, just like anybody else, only I'm not allowed to acknowledge it. I need to put up a front, and it's bullshit, and that's the bottom line.' "

At Home with Himself and His Sexuality

Don, a musician, married, in his late thirties, has arrived at a different place in his sexual life. After many years of exploring his sexuality, Don feels at home with himself and his sexuality. He's spent a lot of time exploring and thinking about it, before he chose his wife.

"There was no way I was going to get trapped always wanting sex outside of marriage," he said. "So I spent lots of time watching the way people handled sex in their lives. I always love to watch the way people turn their sexual partners into demons or gods. Men do it and women do it too. You see a lot of this in the music business where girls are all over the guys, like they're gods or something. What turns women on is power in a guy. For them that translates into security. It's an aphrodisiac. But it doesn't last very long. I used to get turned on by all these women who looked at me like I was so special, but finally, I realized I was just a fantasy to them. That didn't feel so great finally. These women didn't know the first thing about me. After a while it got lonely. What was I? Just a stud? So I let it all go. When I stopped it, I felt like a crack addict that escaped his addiction. Sex and fantasy together are an addiction, and even though I loved the drug, I got off it finally."

Exploring His Fantasy Women

The way Don managed to beat the "addiction," he said,

"Has to do with the power of the woman I'm with now, my wife. She allows me to remain in relationship with some ex-girlfriends. It's totally platonic though, never sexual. I keep in touch with some of the most beautiful women I used to be with, and my wife meets some of them too. That helps a lot."

In this unusual situation, Don doesn't have to feel as if he's completely given up all other women, so his sense of loss and restriction is not as great. Seeing these women as friends also helps dissolve the fantasies he used to have about them.

"I talk to some of them at least once a week. As I do this I get to see how awesome my wife is, and who these women really are too. One of them told me she's finally in a mo-nogamous relationship with her fiancée, and a month later I find out she's screwing her boss. I realized if I was with her, that would have happened to me, too. I'd be miserable be-cause what she would do would be to give me enough of the sex drug to keep me stoned, but never really be there for me."

In staying in touch with these women, Don is actually trying to get free from his addiction to the fantasy aspect of sex—to see the women for who they are, and transfer his sexual feelings to his wife.

"There's a natural tendency in all of us to go for that short-term gratification in every part of our lives," Don continued, "but it creates disasters. You've got to reach the point where you realize that being in a relationship is not necessarily related to passion, romance, or to sex. Being in a relationship is a lot more than sex. What I always keep in mind is that all my great erotic experiences start merging into one big memory and no one woman could never equal it. If I kept thinking about that memory my wife wouldn't have a chance."

Men Need to Know They Please the Woman

Don and his wife also keep their sexual relationship alive and satisfying by,

"Well, talking honestly, guys need to be told they are great looking, have great bodies, the right dimensions, please a woman, are great lovers and really make her happy. My wife does that for me. She tells me and she means it. I've had plenty of experience with other women so I know how to please her, and I do. This pleases me too. We're both happy for it. I have a friend who's married to a woman who is short on acknowledgment, and this bothers him. A guy needs to hear 'you're wonderful in bed, you make me happy. I think you're great.' "

Don is pointing up the strong need he and many men have to be validated in their sexuality and performance. When a woman is not forthcoming about this, some men feel emasculated and cannot perform as well. Many cases of impotence can be remedied with patience and an ongoing dose of true validation and acknowledgment of all parts of the man's self.

Male Sexuality

Male sexuality is complicated and ranges across a broad spectrum of experiences. Because a man has had a few gay experiences does not mean he is gay; because he has been unfaithful does not mean he will never be able to commit; because he has been addicted to fantasy, does not mean that he will not be able to enjoy and maintain a real relationship.

Sexuality is greatly affected by emotions, fantasies, feelings of self-worth, what is going on in other parts of the man's life and in the relationship. It is also an arena in which feelings such as anger, hurt, disappointment and revenge can come into play. Both unfaithfulness and a lack of sexuality in a relationship may simply be the result of upset and withholding because other needs have not been met.

For most men their sexual performance is a strong measure of their identity. Not only does satisfying sexual activity lead to enhanced self-esteem, but the reverse is true as well. High self esteem will allow a man to perform sexually in a way that pleases both his partner and himself.

In this area, more than in others, the partner's appreciation and acknowledgment of the man are of the utmost importance. Many men feel as if their manhood is on the line when they are being sexual. Lovemaking often is a time of vulnerability and fragility. A loving response from the partner can go a very long way.

It is also crucial to overcome embarrassment about sex and learn to communicate openly, to ask for what is needed and enjoyed, and to be willing to give that back in return. This requires time and commitment, establishing an atmosphere where an individual can feel safe and wanted.

Touchstones to Remember

1. Men express many different aspects of themselves through sexuality: love, hate, revenge, conquest, and the need for control.

2. For men, sex is often just sex. Sometimes there is love, but many times, there isn't. For women, sex usually means love. This creates disconnection.

3. Oftentimes, a man feels he can't be faithful to a woman. While in bed with one woman, he'll be thinking of another. Getting steady sex from a woman is a strong inducement to tell her what she wants to hear.

4. Some men are victims of the Whore-Madonna complex, characterizing women into those who are good (the mothers of their children, and Madonnas) and (those who are bad, the ones they can enjoy sex, the whores). This is a reflection of the man's psyche, and not the woman he chooses.

5. For some, sex is simply a game, a way of getting instantaneous satisfaction, fulfilling a fantasy, or

feeling worthwhile. Once this is achieved they're gone.

6. Men need to know they please the woman, that she enjoys and admires every part of him, including his body. He needs to see this in action and also to be told.

7. Many are unfulfilled sexually, unable to tell that to their partners, or ask for what they want and need. It's crucial to take time to make sex important, to communicate honestly what's really happening for you.

8. Men who are in cold marriages and have regular sex on the outside sooner or later realize what a toll this takes upon them, and their feelings of self-respect. Work on what is wrong in the marriage, emotionally, as well. This can very much affect the sexuality.

9. Gay men have the need to be accepted for who they are, and as importantly, to honor and accept themselves.

10. To be vulnerable is incredibly masculine. All men need to allow themselves to feel their sensitive, intuitive side and be able to admit to their partners that they are fragile, vulnerable and need love.

EIGHT

Men and Marriage

Marriage is a complicated issue for most men. There are the women they love, women they bed, women they can be friends with, but the woman they marry is someone else. She's there for the long haul, a person who must play many roles in their life, someone they want to find both comfort and passion with, someone familiar, who makes them feel at home.

Despite their need for adventure and variety, most men want to be married. They feel more secure when a wife and family are backing them up. Having to provide for a family also lends significance to the man—the sense that his life matters, and his efforts benefit others besides himself.

Personal Inventory: Men and Marriage

Group A: Warriors, Heroes, Adventurers
Group B: Lovers, Dreamers, Peter Pans
Group C: Controllers, Perfectionists, Addicts

Group D: Wise Men, Gurus, Seers
Group E: A Regular Guy!

SCORING
(Score each question from 1–4 in the following manner)

1. Not at all
2. Sometimes
3. Often
4. All the time

1. Does he need to be married to someone who is way beyond his reach or gives him trouble at every turn?

2. Is he willing to give up everything to be with the one he loves?

3. Does he insist upon only marrying someone who fits his picture completely of the perfect wife?

4. Is he only interested in marrying someone where there are endless obstacles in their path?

5. Does he long for romance, not so much for marriage?

6. Does he feel as though he is complete as he is and marriage with a specific person is unnecessary?

7. Does he have to constantly call and check up on his wife?

8. Does he choose a woman with whom he is also friends?

9. Is his marriage a constant whirl of ups and downs?

10. Will he wait forever until he meets the right one?

11. Is he able to sacrifice some of his needs to make the marriage work?

12. Does he always have to be right when an argument comes up?

13. Does he see his marriage as a covenant with God?

14. Is he willing to look away from certain of his partner's faults?

15. Does he experience marriage as an enormous trap?

16. Is he marrying a person who will make him look good?

17. Does marriage include lots of time for intimacy and finding out about who his partner really is?

18. Is his mate also a partner in his spiritual experiences?

19. Is marriage a place in which to make his dreams come true?

20. Is the marriage ordained, the workings of destiny?

ANSWERS

Group A: Warriors, Heroes, Adventurers
(Questions 1, 4, 9, 15) Score 12 points or more

These men enjoy challenge, difficulty and adventure in their marriages. If problems do not exist, they create them to spice things up and make the time seem worthwhile. If things are running smoothly, they may feel that the love is gone. The women that make suitable mates for them are usually independent, free thinking, and enjoy adventure as well.

Group B: Lovers, Dreamers, Peter Pans
(Questions 2, 5, 10, 19) Score 12 points or more

These men are more in love with love than with being married and all the hard work it can entail. They create a fantasy about their wives and what marriage is supposed to be. When these fantasies dwindle they feel as though something has gone wrong, or as if they've been deceived. In marriage with these kinds of men, it is crucial to keep the romance going. Plan dates and quality time alone together. Dress romantically and bring candles, wine and soft music into your life as you go along.

Group C: Controllers, Perfectionists, Addicts
(Questions 3, 7, 16, 12) Score 12 points or more

These men must control every aspect of the marriage, often including who the wife sees and where she goes. They can be suspicious and possessive and demand that she give a continual accounting. The wives they choose are most usually amenable to their control. This gives the man a feeling of power, but does not allow the partner to grow. When the partner becomes tired of this arrangement, or does begin to grow, the balance is destroyed and the marriage is in real trouble.

Group D: Wise Men, Gurus, Seers
(Questions 6, 13, 18, 20) Score 12 points or more

While we find a good number of these men unmarried, the ones who are view their unions differently. They see their wives as spiritual partners, consecrated to them in their journey of serving God. Most choose women who are also involved in spiritual practice so that can each support one another in their devotions.

A real guy usually views his marriage partner as his friend as well. They wish a mutual arrangement, where both can learn and grow. He is forgiving of himself and others and able to look aside from some of the faults his partner may have, accepting her as an evolving person who, like him, has room to grow.

A Whole New Dimension

"My marriage gave my life a whole new dimension," said David, a thirty-two-year-old engineer. "This actually surprised me. I had dated for years and was beginning to agree with everyone who thought that I was a confirmed bachelor. I was definitely becoming set in my ways and overly picky about the women I met. But after a while it wasn't too hard for me to recognize that something was missing in my life. How many women can you date? How many eyes can you look into? I guess you might say I was ready for commitment and building something together."

There seems to be an inner timetable for men as well as women, a biological clock of his own which tells them that a committed life with another would make him more, not less of who he is, expand his horizons.

"Of course like everyone else of my generation," David continued, "I was terrified of making a mess of it, terrified of my marriage turning out like my parents, and the parents of most of my friends—divorced. We've all heard plenty of horror stories, enough to keep ourselves from jumping in.

"As well as fear of jumping in," Dave continued, "there's a lot of confusion about who does what these days in marriage, what kind of roles we'll have to play. Lots of women tell you up front they don't expect to be stay-at-home moms, or give up working. Their careers seem to come first to them. Where does that leave us? Some of us feel they're all getting back at us just for being men.

"This scares lots of guys away. They stay single for much longer. They say, 'Who needs to be married to a buddy, or someone who's going to compete with you about how much money you make?' Deep down, guys want to take care of their wives, want to be the breadwinners. Still, at some point or another, most of us want to marry. I'm not exactly sure why."

Basic Need For Home And Family

What we have here is the need for male identity appearing in the arena of relationships. When roles are clear cut, the man has a sense of boundaries, of what is expected of him and what he needs to do to succeed. The primal need to care for his wife and family, to hunt and bring home supplies, to protect the family from outside danger, unconsciously stirs him. When the roles are not clear, the need stirs, but there is more conflict and hesitation about fulfilling it.

Dr. Diane Shainberg, psychologist, therapist, and teacher of meditation says,

"Often men have the concept that there's something wrong with a person if they don't have a mate. Women have it too, but with men it's deeper. There's an onus on a man when he says, 'I don't have anybody,' as if he didn't have himself, or God. Women know this is a conventional, prescriptive conclusion or judgment, and that it's not really true. Whereas, I think men really believe that there is something wrong with a woman who doesn't have a mate as well. They see it as being diseased in some way."

The need to be seen as whole in the eyes of society can be a driving force for both men and women. Aside from the human need for bonding and companionship, being seen as a husband or wife offers social validation that some cannot live without.

"So," David said, "even with all this worry, I still felt something was definitely missing in my life. Being single is fine, but then one day you just have had enough of it. Shortly after I realized I had enough, out of the blue, I met Alice."

Of course David did not meet Alice, his wife to be, out of the blue. He met her because he was psychologically ready to take the next step in his development. He looked at this particular woman differently because he, himself, was open to a new form of relating. He was ready to respond to his need to grow together and be generative, to build a new family unit to repair whatever damage he experienced in his original family. Consciously or unconsciously, David was ready to make a new family, the kind he'd always wanted.

"It was funny," David continued, "as soon as I met Alice, I felt I could trust her. We fit together easily. She was less concerned with her career for one thing, and more concerned with me. She looked up to my accomplishments, too. That felt wonderful. Within a few months I was pretty certain that she was the one for me. She said she knew on the second or third date. Women are funny that way."

It's interesting how many men, and women too, seem to know quite early on in the relationship that this person is going to be their mate. A different level of connection and recognition seems to take place. Also, there is usually a deeper level of comfort and trust.

"We've been married three years now, and although it's not always easy, it's basically good. I'm glad we're together. I'm a bigger person with her, more grounded and secure. We're expecting our first child two months from now. That's bonding us even more. Sometimes she wakes me up at night and says she's scared and asks me to just hold her. I like doing that. It makes me feel important.

"Do I miss dating? Sometimes I'd rather go hang with the guys, too, but all in all, this marriage is fine. I'm proud I can do it. I didn't know if I could."

Although men are marrying later these days, put off by the examples of their parents' marriages, the high cost of living and lack of clarity about the roles to be played, once they've actually taken the step, many feel relieved and happy. Although some say marriage is an antiquated institution, the basic human need for home, family, trust and ongoing relatedness makes marriage a crucial hallmark in a man's life.

Lewis Harrison was married for the first time in his forties, after being with countless women. Marriage was something he had been waiting and preparing for his whole life long. Lewis says,

"I always wanted what I have. I wanted to be with a woman who wouldn't give me a lot of grief. All the others gave me a lot of grief. When she does give me grief I let her know. I'm working, she's not. I'm supporting us so I feel, why is she giving me grief? But the truth is I don't want her to go get a job, because I like having her around. So, she's giving me a lot by being here."

Lewis is able to both recognize and acknowledge what his wife brings to him and the relationship. He also is able to accept the fact that he wants and likes to have her around. This is fairly unusual for most men, who might see this as dependency, or feel that by her not working too much burden was resting upon them. Having been single for so long prepared Lewis to appreciate what he is now receiving.

After his marriage he discovered some new things about his wife too. He says, "I think the percentage of stuff that I like and don't like about her is the same. Some of the particular items change, but the percentage remains. I'm aware I have to live with all parts of a person, whether I like them or not. That's a main component of marriage."

Being able to accept both his wife's negative and positive aspects is another expression of his maturity and comes from years of relating to all kinds of women.

Don't Always Worry about Balancing the Scales

"Personally, I like the idea of compromise," Lewis continued, "but people don't compromise—they say they do, but they don't. If they're wise, in marriage, they pick their battles carefully, and surrender a lot. And you have your bottom lines. If your bottom lines are not met, you're going to be miserable. So, as an example of what I do about this is, say she wants to watch a particular show that I don't want to watch, first, I get off it and let her watch the show. Then I say I'd like to put some music on, and she says, I'd like quiet now. So, it can be hard—we don't live in a huge apartment. So, what I've learned to do, is I have a small walkman, and I play my music on that. It works. That's what I mean by compromising—finding ways to live with these differences in peace."

Lewis is not counting who is giving what to who. He concedes that he may be the one primarily compromising, but says,

"As I see it, *marriage is primarily about giving. Think what you can give, not what you're getting.* You're getting enough. Don't worry about it. Don't always worry about balancing the scales. For example, I don't think I'm very eccentric but everyone else I speak to says I don't even have a clue about how eccentric I am. And they're probably right. In fact, in my forty-eight years I have not met a woman who would marry me. So, this can't be so easy for my wife either. Whatever it is about me, though, my wife isn't bothered by it. That's a great gift to me. And she isn't a materialistic person. She always tells me how nice it would be to be wealthy, but she doesn't do a whole lot to make it happen and doesn't give me much grief for not doing too much either. She's okay with the way things are."

Lewis is extremely appreciative of the ways his wife does not put pressure on him. He has adopted a large view of his wife, himself and marriage, is able to see it in context, not get derailed by the small issues as they arise. This ability to see the whole picture may be a crucial aspect to the ability to forgive and move on.

Don't Let Each Other's Limitations Impede You

"What we have," Lewis continued, "is mutual acceptance of each other. That works as long as you don't let the other one's limitations impede you. That's part of the work of marriage. It means you go out driving at night even though she can't. I don't really want to go without her, but if I have to, I will. She'll go with me most of the time. The tip is for me not to give her grief about her initial response. So I say, 'If you don't drive with me, I'm going to really miss you. But, I'm driving up Tuesday night. The bus leaves from the Port Authority Wednesday morning. Take it and call me when you get there and I'll pick you up at the bus station.' Mostly she goes."

By understanding his wife's psychological dynamics, and not allowing them to manipulate or constrict him, Lewis relates to her strengths, not her weaknesses, and in this processes empowers her as well.

If You Want to Be Married, You Make It Work

"If you want to be married, you make it work. If you don't want to be married, it doesn't work. You can find a million reasons. Whenever someone tells me they grew apart, I don't know what to really make of that."

It may be that men leave their marriages because they haven't lived through all the relationships that Lewis had a chance to explore all the years of being single.

"Longing for different relationships can be a strong drug," he said. "Especially when things go wrong, you want that drug. It's what your inner, demented thirteen-year-old wants. And what is it that the little kid inside really wants? I'll tell you what these fantasies usually come down to. Here it goes: she's someone with the greatest body in the world—every other guy wants her, but she only wants me and tells me so. And, she's economically independent, but wants to spend all her time with me. And she's very intellectual, has a great sense of style, but is not attached to fashion, and we sit around in bed reading the Sunday *Times* and talking about Kafka. She knows the six hundred and thirteen laws of the Torah by heart and has a rational commentary about why it looks like she's breaking the laws, but really isn't. And it makes sense. She meditates a lot. And she'd be selfless too. And no calluses on her feet. And she'd be predictable and manageable, controllable and she would love all my worst qualities. She'd love me even when I haven't shaved for a day. Is that too much to ask?"

Lewis laughed loudly. "These are the ridiculous fantasies that can ruin fine marriages." He keeps laughing because, at this point, he realizes these fantasies don't hold up. He has found, in his marriage, his wife, and himself, something real and solid.

Give Up the Fantasy

"In order to be in a relationship," Lewis continued, "the first thing you have to do is know that you want other fantasies and then give it up. This is the truth about being satisfied where you now are. There's a book, the hundred greatest romances in history—but none of these people were married, it's just the greatest romances in history. Cleopatra and Mark Anthony. Romeo and Juliet—wait a minute, she committed suicide. The greatest marriages in history are boring. Hey, honey, can you pass the cereal?"

In many ways Lewis is unusual. Not all men have come to this kind of deep understanding of the dynamics of relationship. Not many can recognize and give up the fantasies that drive them, seeing them for what they are. How many are willing to focus on giving, rather than receiving? For this, and reasons like this, men can feel trapped in marriages with no way of getting free.

Longing for Love In a Marriage

Fred, a low-key, pleasant, sensitive family man longs for his wife and longs for things to be good between them for awhile. He longs for sexual fulfillment in the marriage, where he and many men like him, feel starved.

"My wife is a dancer," Fred states, "a very serious dancer, who has been on Broadway and in many plays. The relationship between us is very bad. She has always been erratic in her attention to the family and to me. Most of the time she is unavailable sexually as well. She wants me to be more forceful and dynamic and is attracted to men who are like that. What I can't tell her is I'm very frustrated sexually, and the undermining of my sexual desirability just creates even more feelings of worthlessness in me. I've been very depressed. I don't want to leave the family. She's left a few times to develop her career and left me with the children. When she came back (because she wasn't successful), she would be very warm for a short time. Then things would disintegrate again. I don't want this anymore. This life is not satisfying for me, but we have a new, young daughter now, and this leaves me with the additional responsibility of another ten or twelve years out of my life with a woman who's not responsive to me."

Fred's marriage is a jail—a jail of unfulfilled longing, and also a place where he suffers humiliation. One of the strong reasons he tells himself that he stays, however, is because of his unwillingness to leave his little daughter behind. He wants to provide her with a family unit.

"I also know my wife's been having affairs," he continues. "I won't have an affair myself. I would like to, and fantasize about it, and have actually had something with someone on the Internet. For months this person on the Internet and I have been close, but when she wanted to meet me I said I couldn't do it, because I don't want to leave my wife."

There is a masochistic element in Fred's maintaining a relationship in which he is being continually humiliated, left, and deprived of his basic needs. After a long period of being in a situation like this, an individual's self-esteem can become so damaged that they do not believe they can attract, or are worthy of anything else.

Rather than deal with the effects of this situation upon him, Fred keeps hoping for things to change. He dreams of their working it out. Still, as time goes on and these difficulties persist, his sense of self-worth and loveability is diminishing.

I Want to Get Out but Can't Do It

"If I were a forceful person I could break it up and take the kids and get something for myself. I want to get out, but can't do it. I don't want to be responsible for breaking up the family. Part of me keeps hoping I'll get through to her and we'll have a better relationship, but I know it's not true. Whatever advice my therapist gives me on taking a stand, and asking for what I want, goes on deaf ears. I can't do it. There's a crippled part of me and I know it."

Sensitive men often experience themselves as wounded or crippled when they are not able to be "forceful" enough to leave a bad situation, or put the woman in her place. The fear of loss and separation is intense in these cases, as is super-ego conscience and guilt. Fred still feels the family is together, even though he's paying a terrible price. This price is more bearable to him than feeling he caused pain to his children and wife.

"But I also think I'm not alone," said Fred. "I believe many men in their forties who have families are very starved sex-ually. There is a frequency issue, and also a feeling of not being attractive to their wives. Women just don't realize how important it is to a man to feel potent and desirable to them. Why can't someone tell them? What are they thinking?"

In commenting on this issue, Dr. Selwyn Mills, psychol-ogist and leader of men's groups, says,

"I'd say our society for years has emasculated many men, created those like Fred who fear being strong and forceful, equating this with being hurtful instead. I think the advent of feminism has done damage to the nature of male identity in the context of marriage. In terms of single life, it hasn't done much either. In terms of family, the male role has been confused at best and deprecated also in terms of all our publicity and media entertainment. We see men as the foils in the sitcoms, seldom as heroes. The women are the heroes. This permeates a whole attitude about men. Men have picked it up and are acting it out.

"You see this pattern particularly among the working-class groups where there's been a loss in the manufacturing industry. The women all go to work and have to. Some are better educated than the men. These relationships are based on the woman having to work and the male finding it hard to help with domestic chores because they are tied into a more traditional model of marriage. So, in many of these relationships, after the romance wears off, the men hang out in bars and in packs, go hunting and to football games, ignoring their wives and hating women because they don't have the respect they need. The propensity for physical violence has risen tremendously, especially in these men and others, and the huge increase of domestic abuse in our society is the outcome."

Domestic Abuse and Powerlessness In Men

It is interesting to look at the rise of domestic abuse in connection with feelings of powerlessness among men. In some cases, girlfriend and spouse abuse may be the only way these men know to regain a sense of power and control, to prove their male dominance. A challenge our society faces is to find a way for men to feel empowered in their masculinity and channel and express their aggression in constructive ways.

All men are not aggressive. There is a difference between being assertive, ambitious, focussed and aggressive. Aggression implies the wish to harm another, assaulting another due to personal frustrations and feelings of weakness. For some men seeing that they can harm another is a sign of their strength and power. The only real way to remedy this is to help these men discover their true strength, power and value. A man who is truly satisfied with himself and his life will not have to harm anybody. On the contrary, he will want to share with others and empower them as well.

Aggression crops up in different forms. Abuse is not only physical, but can be expressed in a relationship emotionally and sexually, like depriving the partner of love, or carrying on an ongoing affair with someone else.

Unfaithfulness in a Marriage

Bob, a successful businessman in his early fifties, married for almost eighteen years, has a woman in her thirties who he sees three or four times a week on the side. His wife goes about her business, and they don't talk a lot.

"Every time I approach my wife sexually," he says, "she pushes me away. She suspects I'm having an affair but won't ask me directly and I won't tell her. I'm not even happy with the affair. I'm not in love with that woman either—she's only a diversion to me. I haven't had sex in a long time with my wife, so she's there for that. She wants me to leave my wife and I won't. I've started drinking too. In a sense, I'm headed for a disaster. With the drinking and the affair, I feel my life will blow up at any time, and almost want it to."

When no other way is seen out of a bad situation, some men create a time bomb to explode in their lives. They unconsciously feel this explosion can end the marriage for them, can open a door they can't find any other way through.

"I've been going to a therapist about this for a year. He's stopped me from committing suicide, anyway. The wife comes to therapy too. She says she thinks I'm having an affair but, of course, I won't admit to it. So, what's the use of therapy? The therapist doesn't push me to tell her. The whole situation is at loggerheads now."

Most therapists would help Bob to confront and discuss the truth about what's going on with his wife. The most crucial aspect of marriage is the trust and honesty between the partners. When that has been compromised, there is never anywhere further to go. No matter how much pain, hurt and humiliation would emerge from a clear airing of the truth here, it would be better than this ongoing lie they are living with, which stops all possibilities for repair or change.

"The wife and I are angry with each other constantly," Bob continues. "When we go out socially, we go with big cars and expensive clothes. Our friends are other couples who are just as unhappy as we are. We're all putting on a big show for each other about how happy and successful we are, about how we made it. Still I need the married life. I couldn't make it single, living on the fringe, alone."

Unfortunately, there are many couples who live the married life that Bob describes. They cling to the show and the social security the marriage provides, pretending to live wonderful lives. They find it easier to stay in an established routine and feel as though they are part of the mainstream, than to face what is going on and repair it, or if necessary, start all over again. As this goes on over time, as the falseness of the situation deepens and any hope of addressing the issues fades, and people often feel trapped in such hopelessness that suicidal feelings can arise.

In some cases the anger between the couple can also be felt as a bond, one which replaces true intimacy. It can be harder to leave someone you are so angry with, than someone you can talk with and feel more neutral toward. Not only does anger create a tremendous bond, but you can want to stay there and make them pay.

For some, it is safer to be angry with the person they live with than to be close, and have feelings of love. The anger provides a boundary for them. And, if they are feeling so much anger, too much cannot be demanded of them. This can make them feel free of certain responsibilities to one another, and provides justification for living any kind of life they wish.

Bob is clinging to an unreal marriage, unreal social life and an unreal self. Living in this unreality has caused the hollowness which has gripped his entire life. This is the inevitable outgrowth of a life based upon lies and games, where there is no respect or integrity with the other person or with oneself. Marriage takes courage. Relationships require truth and the ability to grow up, give up our toys, and reach for that which is real.

Deep Secrets in a Marriage

Some live for years with deep secrets their partners never dream of. Not only does this build silent walls, it prevents the man from ever fully being present and becomes a way of keeping a separate self that the wife may never know of.

Roger, a warm, affable man in his mid-fifties, has been happily married for twenty-two years and yet is living with a deep secret.

"I'm very happy with my marriage," he said, "but what I've got to tell you is that I've always been in love with my wife's sister. Now, don't get me wrong, I have a beautiful wife and I love her—I've been a great husband too. I have two beautiful daughters and I love them. I love my mother-in-law. I've been a great father and son-in-law. I've done my best for everyone, but I've always secretly adored my wife's sister. This has been a source of great pain for me. Her sister is married and I like her husband as well. In fact, the four of us socialize regularly. But, everytime she walks into the room, my life lights up. This started happening shortly after I married. I began realizing that she was really the one for me. It's funny though, I'm not unhappy with my wife—actually I'm happy with her."

What is particularly disturbing about this situation is that it has been going on for years. Although Roger claims to love his wife, all along he has been longing for her sister. Should his wife find out about this, she might certainly feel betrayed not only by the depth of his feelings, but by the fact that he never told her, or gave her a chance to decide what she wanted to do under these circumstances.

A Man Can Love More than One Woman at a Time

Roger, however, does not feel there is anything wrong with what has been going on. "What I want to say is that a man can love more than one woman at a time. It's a myth to think that you can only love one woman. I love my wife. I care about her. I'd give my life for her tomorrow—but she doesn't affect me the way her sister does."

Roger feels that he is able to love two women, and that it is probably natural for a man to do so. His feelings toward the sister are highly romantic, filled with intense emotion. It is often difficult, if not impossible, to maintain this level of feeling toward the woman you are married to, and interact with daily, in many mundane capacities. Distance is usually needed to project the romantic fantasy.

When a situation seems impossible, when it seems as though you can never have the person, this can become the perfect soil for romantic fantasies to flourish. All through history and literature we see the greatest romantic longings and fantasies develop in situations where the lovers are starcrossed, or for profound reasons, unable to ever get together. This keeps the love in the realm of fantasy, where it does not have to be tested in the everyday world, and can therefore always remain pristine and strong.

Fantasy is an integral part of romantic and sexual relationships. It is inevitable that a man will meet different people along the way who will stimulate certain fantasies and longings. When these are not acted upon, they can be channeled into his present relationship. It is different, however, when a man finds himself fantasizing consistently about another. That would indicate there is something missing in his life situation, some deep need going unmet. In this case, it would be beneficial for Roger to understand what it is he is longing for, discuss it, and try to work it through with his partner.

In order to keep fantasy and romance alive in a longstanding marriage, the two individuals have to work at it. They must counteract the natural forces of gravity which cause marriage partners to see each other in a more mundane manner. Romantic dates together, vacations, time alone, gifts, and sometimes even a little distance, so they can miss each other, all help keep the fire alive.

"All these years," Roger continued, "whenever I see my wife's sister, my dreams are inspired, I sleep better at night,

I'm thrilled. And I have to tell you that I dream that one day her husband will pass away and my wife will pass away, and we'll finally get together. Now I don't know if my wife has any idea about how I feel, but I believe her sister does.

"One night at the end of August, I wrote her a letter. It was during a thunderstorm. I was feeling romantic and couldn't contain myself any longer. The four of us had gone away for a long weekend together at Lake George, a cabin near the lake, and I saw her standing there after the rain ended in the misty night. I rushed into the cabin and wrote her a love poem. Her husband wasn't there right then, so I went out later and slipped it under her cabin door. Then I watched from my window. I could see her read the letter. I saw that she was upset, and realized then that she felt as I did."

Roger finally could not contain himself, and expressed his feelings toward his sister-in-law. Although he saw her read the note, there is no way he could know how she really was feeling. He projected his wishes upon her in this instance, as in many others that must have taken place.

"She never said a word about the note," Roger went on. "In fact, she acted as though she never got the letter, even though, of course, I know she did. That was a few years ago. But now that I'm getting older and my children are getting older, the longing is greater to leave my wife and run off with her. I feel that she feels that way too. Is it possible that it will happen? Doubtful. But if she gave me just one little sign of encouragement, I would come forward and say to her, 'Elaine, let's go.'

"I love my wife and children, but is marriage a life sentence? Enough is enough. Now I want Elaine. Elaine never had any children, she never could. Of course she loves our children, she's a wonderful aunt. But she could be more than an aunt. She could be a true beloved to me. And someday she may."

Roger lives in a world of his own making with regard to Elaine. The fact that she never responded to him in any way shows that she simply could not cope with his message. She may have been horrified or frightened. At any rate, there is little likelihood that the situation will change.

A great deal of the strength of Roger's feelings and fantasy about Elaine seems to be that it is very unlikely that this relationship can ever come to fruition. There would be so many painful consequences if it actually took place, that, in a way, he is safe to dream of her. This ongoing dream of Elaine fills up the void he feels in his own marriage, and in his own life. It can also serve as an enormous energy drain, and prevent him from being and giving all he can to others in his life as well.

"I feel no guilt," Roger said. "I feel richer in my heart for the fact that I've been able to have this extra love. I don't believe that it is intended to have one love a whole life long. Maybe the penguins do that, but we are human beings. If I ever had the opportunity to go off with Elaine, why would it have to spoil the wonderful years I gave to my wife and children? Now I need something else."

This *deep love* Roger found has never been tested, except in the arena of his own mind, where Elaine can do no wrong. Should he take this fantasy out into everyday life, and have to deal with the realities of her responses to him, he might feel very differently. It is crucial here to distinguish between *love* and *fantasy*. Fantasy breeds intense feeling, intoxication, and people who seem larger than life. Love is a deep abiding bond which never goes away. It is proven by time and in time, no matter how buffeted, grows deeper day by day.

The Law of the Heart

"I am begging for someone to understand how I feel and not to think I'm a horrible person," Roger said. "Sometimes I feel like a monster, but I know I'm not. I know God didn't intend for me to be only with one person. That view is man-made, and for some of us it's against the law of our heart.

"The question of my life is, will I have the courage to actually go to her and say, 'Elaine, the time has come'? I think of that every night. What do you think? Would I be destroying my children and wife? Why would it have to be that way? Why couldn't they have big hearts too and say you loved us, you gave to us, now go and take something you want so badly for yourself?"

Of course Roger realizes that his family would most likely not be able to do this. Very few would. Most likely they would feel deeply betrayed. Because he realizes how they would actually feel, he at times considers himself a monster. Although he longs to live in a world where all could feel as he did, and give him permission to act on his fantasy, another part of him recognizes how unlikely this is. The strength of this persistent fantasy has made him wish to blot out other realities as well.

When he considered whether or not others would feel betrayed, he said,

"But the question is, am I betraying my own self and my own heart by not saying, 'Elaine, I love you and want to leave with you'? I don't know the answer myself. But I don't want to live the rest of my life waiting for my wife to die or for Elaine's husband to die. We are different people at different times in our lives, our needs change, our values change, we grow differently. Why can't we face it and make room for that change? My wife and I shared something beautiful. Why should it ruin those years because now I need something different?"

Roger's questions arise from a place inside that is in a great deal of pain. He is fighting with his feelings and with the social structure. It is also very likely that this obsession with Elaine is a displacement for other pain he has in his life, that he is unaware of. His incredible longing for that which he cannot have may well date back to childhood, where he experienced deep deprivation of a loved one, or other traumatic situation that never got resolved.

When faced with similar feelings, some men choose to leave the marriage and start a new life. Others remain. Both choices have consequences. A third choice, of deep self-exploration and understanding, seems the wisest at this juncture.

In Roger's situation he needs to confront his feelings, dreams, wishes, marriage and personal history straight on. Rather than running from one relationship to another, he needs to understand how he could have allowed this fantasy to run wild for so many years. He must come to grips with what is truly lacking in his life, what is really going on between him and his wife. Although fantasies seem silent and private, their effects upon us can be felt by those we come into contact with.

Don't Hold Back

Rabbi Gelberman, a wonderful eighty-seven-year-old interfaith rabbi, has married and counseled many about how to make marriages grow, and about the differences between a lasting union and a fantasy.

"When man meets woman and woman meets man," says Rabbi Gelberman, "and there is a special feeling between them, from that very moment, they're holding back. Why? Because they fear the other person will find out something that isn't good about them. Naturally, they want to hide that, at least until they get married. This creates the problem. This is why so many come home from the honeymoon and say, 'Who's this person I married? I'm in shock.' "

Many marry the person they dream of and not the one who is really there. Sooner or later, the realities of who they have will hit them. It is far better to reveal your whole self to your partner before the wedding takes place. Some believe that once married, they can change the other or themselves. This is never the basis of a relationship. Marriage is not a cure all that automatically makes things work out.

"As modern as I am, I believe the old way of finding your mate is better," said Rabbi Gelberman. "Why? Let me tell you. For my first marriage, I never knew my wife. We met under the Chuppah (the bridal canopy). The parents knew each other, they were of the same background, religion, the same philosophy, the same customs, everything the same, except we didn't know about each other as people."

Meeting to determine attraction wasn't necessary.

"We saw photographs. It wasn't such a big deal. If she looked all right, what's the problem? So then we got married, and the next day I found out one or two things about her that I wondered about. But the very same day I also found out five things that were wonderful, that I knew nothing about before. By the time the day ended, it evened itself out.

"But in our modern society, we know all the good things about each other, but none of the bad. So, during the honeymoon, we find out all of the bad. That makes it difficult to overcome. The first thing I tell people who want to get married is to be honest with each other, whatever you're holding back, tell it now. It's better to lose now, than to lose later. But fear is the greatest enemy in everything. Often they tell me, 'This was the love of the century,' and it was. But they didn't know each other. So what was it that they loved?"

As in the case of Roger above, these individuals who thought they found the love of their lives, were most likely projecting their own dreams, wishes and visions upon the other person, without knowing who they really were. Due to the ongoingness of marriage, this state of projection cannot last. Sooner or later, the man must wake up.

"When there's trouble, I tell them to find out what brought them together, and re-create it now. For most it's hard to remember, because they didn't know in the first place."

Acts of Love

Rabbi Gelberman is touching upon the crucial question of what it is that inspires love. What is it that we are hoping for when we dedicate ourselves to a mate? When trouble begins in a marriage, it is easy to forget. By doing acts of love, no matter how we are feeling, it is easy to build a bridge of love once again. By watching our tongue, offering forgiveness, stopping to listen, letting go of our expectations, we are offering acts of love.

Marriage itself is a practice in which we are being given the opportunity to grow. In order to do this, it is crucial to focus more upon giving more than receiving as the marriage continues. Most do not do this. "Men look at marriages like a business deal, they see love as comfort. This can be a terrible mistake."

This is an interesting distinction. Many men see marriage as a refuge from the hard-edged life of business and competition, a place for succor and comfort. However, the experience of love is not always of comfort. Love and marriage can be challenging to the extreme, stirring up fears of loss and inadequacy. Although men may have great love affairs, often that woman does not become their wife. Most cannot tolerate that level of intensity for a lifetime. A lot of disappointment and anger in a marriage arises from different expectations, or definitions of what a marriage is for.

"The truth of the matter is that it is difficult to live with anyone, and we have to compromise," said Rabbi Gelberman. "So, if you see a fire, isn't it your job to make sure it's put out? But usually each person just adds to the fire. Be careful. Be silent when angry. Put out a fire the minute you see it. What you say in anger is so hurtful. It's hard to forget."

Although it is important to express yourself in a marriage, to let your partner know what upsets you, what makes you angry and hurt, timing is everything. It is best not to communicate when you are in a state of anger or pain. Your words will inevitably be intended not to heal wounds, but to lash out. The intention behind your communication is of the utmost importance. When the heat of anger has dissolved and both partners are able to listen thoughtfully is the best time to share your feelings and needs.

Respect What Is Important to the Other

"I know another couple, and the wife is very much into cleanliness. Her husband is not clean enough for her, though he's clean. So, even though it doesn't mean that much for him, he has to respect what it means to her. A marriage that is not based on respect for what is important to the other cannot last. To him it's silly, but to the other it isn't. There's a beautiful saying in the Pier Ki Avot; *'Don't judge your fellow man until you are in his place.'* You must put yourself in your mate's place. Respect that they have a right to care about what it is they care about."

Rabbi Gelberman is speaking about the ultimate foundation of marriage—allowing the other to be who he is, and giving respect. So often we are able to love and respect an individual who seems to be a mirror of ourselves, or to have qualities and virtues we admire. This is not really loving or respecting another, but a form of narcissism, loving ourselves.

Marriage requires that we grow. It is beneficial to focus upon the positive aspects of our partner, to keep relating to his strength, not weakness. Yet, sooner or later, we will have to face qualities in our partner which are different from our own, perhaps aspects of the person that we do not like. It is crucial to understand that our role is not to be judge and jury. Our partner does not exist simply to satisfy us. Each person is unique and has the right to be who they are. We must learn to allow differences and respect qualities other than our own.

We need to become able to put ourselves in our partner's place, and feel what he is going through. When a person feels truly understood, and not judged, change often happens by itself.

Sacrifice Is Not Understood

In our society, the idea of sacrifice in marriage is largely outmoded. In fact, sacrifice of any kind is not understood. People believe that sacrifice will not make anyone happy, just guilty. However, true sacrifice, is a gift to both the giver and receiver.

Today, we are taught to make ourselves happy first, and others will benefit from this. The real question is whether or not a person has the faintest idea of what real happiness is. Does happiness consist of instant gratification, or the fulfillment of every desire? Belief in instant satisfaction forces an individual to become a slave to his passing feelings.

The concept of accepting all aspects of a person and situation is also outmoded. In our demand for personal pleasure and gratification, we don't develop the ability to accept all aspects of life's experiences. However, marriage itself, if it is to endure, demands that we learn this. The Jewish religion says that when two people get married it is not because they are at the peak of their love—it is marriage itself which will *teach* them how to love. Their marriage partner is their teacher. How many now view marriage that way?

Marriage is a sacred trust between two individuals, a place where both can feel safe, honored, nurtured and have the ability to develop themselves in whatever way they are called to. It is not a place for constriction, possessiveness, punishment, or the feeling one has to constantly please the other, or all is lost. The willingness to respect the other unconditionally, to offer forgiveness, to give the other the room to grow and change, allows the marriage to endure through time as a pliable, living organism which will nurture both parties.

Touchstones to Remember.

1. Most men want to be married. They feel more secure with a wife and family backing them up.

2. A man marries when he's ready to take the next step in his development, when he looks at a woman differently.

3. Don't always worry about balancing the scales. Marriage is primarily about giving. Think about what you're giving, not what you're getting all the time.

4. Pick your battles carefully, and surrender a lot. Don't let the other person's limitations impede you. Respect where they're at, but honor yourself as well.

5. If a man wants to be married, he has to make it work. He must give up old fantasies and realize that they are only dreams.

6. Feelings of powerlessness in men stimulates abuse of all kinds—physical, mental and emotional. A man needs to respect himself in marriage, and feel needed and strong.

7. Some men can and do love more than one woman at a time. These men become torn between the laws of society and the laws of their heart.

8. Don't hold back before marriage. Let the person know who you really are. Don't pretend to be someone you aren't.

9. Respect what is important to the other and don't judge your partner until you are standing in his/her place.

10. True sacrifice is a gift, given with a willing heart. There is no guilt or price tag included. True sacrifice for another is part of long-standing love.

NINE

Men and Spirituality (Heroes, Visions, and Dreams)

"If every tip of every hair on me could speak,
I still couldn't say my gratitude.
In the middle of these streets and gardens I say,
I wish everyone could know what I know."
                                    —*Jalal Al-Din Rumi*

The involvement in, and hunger for spirituality has become more acute over the past ten years. As the number of individuals on anti-depressants increases, as families fall apart, aggression escalates, and young people feel more at a loss, there is a search for deeper values that can bring meaning and comfort to lonely hearts and troubled souls. Along with the traditional forms of spirituality, we see a burgeoning of many alternative paths and practices. For some, spirituality comes through churches, synagogues and mosques. For others workshops, recovery groups, and meditation practices can provide a new life direction and experience of clarity regarding the direction of their lives. What most agree about is that true spirituality involves daily practice. It is not something to be dabbled in.

Personal Inventory: Men and Spirituality

Group A: Warriors, Heroes, Adventurers
Group B: Lovers, Dreamers, Peter Pans
Group C: Controllers, Perfectionists, Addicts
Group D: Wise Men, Gurus, Seers
Group E: A Real Guy!

SCORING
(Score each question from 1–4 in the following manner)

1. Not at all
2. Sometimes
3. Often
4. All the time

1. Does he enjoy spending time with himself?

2. Is he rigid in his beliefs about life?

3. Does he feel life is a huge quest that he must make?

4. Does he find the greatest fulfillment with someone he loves?

5. Is quiet time crucial to him? Does he make sure he has this, no matter what?

6. Is he an independent thinker?

7. Does he constantly seek perfection?

8. Is he open to new truths and information, always ready to find something out?

9. Does he spend quality time with nature?

10. Is he involved in tasks and projects to benefit the world at large?

11. Does he speak the truth easily, no matter who is there? Can he make room for others to be who they are?

12. Does he find the most joy in life in relationships?

13. Does he always look for and find the beauty in everyone?

14. Is it natural for him to give of himself when others are in need?

15. Is he always seeking something he never can find?

16. Does he feel there is only one way a person can know and serve God?

17. Does he judge others when they do not go along with his ideas about life?

18. Is he open and inviting to all aspects of life?

19. Can he give kindness fully when it is needed?

20. Does he feel finding God is an adventure he delights in?

ANSWERS

Group A: Warriors, Heroes, Adventurers
Questions (3, 10, 15, 20) Score 12 points or more

For these men, spirituality involves great adventure, conquering new dimensions, putting themselves in exotic places, finding teachers, having the great courage to take the inner journey and discover who they truly are. They often go against common wisdom and mainstream values in forging new visions to live by.

Group B: Lovers, Dreamers, Peter Pans
Questions (4, 12, 9, 13) Score 12 points or more

These men find their spirit awakening often in the experience of love, and surrender to the object of their love. Spiritually speaking, their lives are based on devotion, service and deep union with their beloved. In this experience their sense of self expands to provide them a sense of great meaning and joy.

Group C: Controllers, Perfectionists, Addicts
Questions (2, 7, 16, 17) Score 12 points or more

These men initially find it difficult to surrender, or acknowledge a power greater than themselves. When their form of lifestyle has taken its toll of them, some eventually relinquish their need to be omnipotent, give up their craving for power and control, and in yielding to the flow of life, or to a higher power, often find the cure for their addiction and loneliness.

Group D: Wise Men, Gurus, Seers
(Questions 1, 14, 18, 19) Score 12 points or more

These individuals live their entire lives dedicated to spirituality, to serving God or a higher purpose, and being present and available to all of life. Without this orientation they see no reason for being here at all.

Group E: A Real Guy
(Questions 5, 6, 8, 11) Score 12 points or more

These men attempt to live a life of authenticity and integrity in the pursuit of values they consider important. They are usually honest in their personal dealings, generous and able to be depended upon.

Working On Yourself Daily

Joel, a fifty-five-year-old businessman has been doing spiritual practice for many, many years. He sees it as daily work, nothing special now, part of the routine.

"Working on yourself spiritually is daily work," Joel says. "It happens slowly. You do it one day, then the next day, you just keep it up. Things grow slowly. You build your muscles."

Most view spirituality as consisting of certain feelings, insights or perceptions that come and go in a flash. They do not realize that true spirituality has to be worked at, nurtured and practiced on a daily basis. It takes time to integrate wisdom with all aspects of your life.

"Some people think you do one thing and then you're a new person," Joel said. "This has been a twenty-seven-year journey for me. The real spiritual recovery came more for me from the twelve-step program than anything else. This program met my needs because there's an articulation of what's going on in your life, how you're being false.

"I also meditate. In meditation you're not being false, you're being your Self, there's no talking things over, no shame, guilt, concept of right and wrong. Just being. That's good, and it's important, but in recovery you work on the wrongs you've done and make amends. You turn your life over to a Higher Power, and in this way are retraining yourself. There are real similarities in all the paths. The Torah speaks of kindness, Christianity speaks of love, Buddhism speaks of compassion. They're all the same."

Joel is describing different aspects of practice, different ways of working with our lives. There is time for reflection, confession, and discussion with others. There is also a need for meditation, time to face oneself alone, and work silently with the deepest parts of oneself.

"What is really most important to me, the real test of who you are, is your relationship with others," Joel said. "That's what makes you healthy. Like today, I went to the supermarket to get a few things. I gave the guy my credit card, and he had the worst time getting the paper in. I made a few jokes about it and made him feel better. But so many times in my life if people had little problems like that, it would bother me. I'd be thinking bad things about them in my mind. This way is much better. I felt good when I left and so did he."

For Joel, relationships, and the small daily events that confront us are also a place for practice. They give us an opportunity to respond differently, and are a true measure and test of where we are really at.

> "I find, in relationships, you're better off listening, taking it all in, not pushing with your needs. It's easy to talk about this, but hard to walk the talk. As I see it, the meditation makes it easier to walk the talk. There's no talk in meditation really, so you just walk the walk.
>
> "Meditation is the realization of no ego. It's the ego in life that's the killer, not only of others, but of my own body. People think that the ego is their identity, so they cling to it. And commercial society reinforces that with messages like get revenge, sex, money, power. Movies and television all show us a guy having a good time and he's rich and wealthy. The society doesn't realize that these messages make us sick rather than healthy. Meditation is taking time to stop and see the effect these messages have on us, and learning how to tune out those that are toxic."

For Joel, spiritual work has to include the mind, heart, body and soul. It gives him the power to sort out his own values, and reject that which may be prevalent, but which is toxic in his life. All aspects of life must be involved in spiritual efforts, and the fruits of the work a man does will be reflected in the quality of his relationships, not only with those that are near and dear, but with all. This is reminiscent of a famous Jewish saying, "If you want to know what spiritual level a Rabbi is on, take a look at how he treats his wife."

Spirituality Is Knowing Your Mission

Dr. Winn Henderson, who dedicates his life to helping others recover from addiction of all kinds, comes from the

Christian tradition, where he had a strong experience of grace and guidance in his life. For him, spirituality is knowing your mission in life, why God put you here, what is expected of you, and what you have to give back.

"If you really believe you're a child of God," Dr. Henderson said, "and if you know that your spiritual father is God and that you have spiritual characteristics that come from that side of your family, just as you have physical characteristics that come from the physical side of the family, and you know God is perfect, you realize that part of you is perfect. If you really believe that, you can't feel that you're worthless, or not worth taking care of. You realize you must do everything that will improve your time here. Before I came to this understanding, I'd just jump in my car, crank it up, and drive down the street. Now I can't feel comfortable about driving anymore until I put on the seat belt, because if I don't, I don't really think I'm important enough to save and protect."

For Dr. Henderson, a true spiritual outlook allows a person to value themselves and take proper care of themselves and others. If a person truly sees their relationship to God, they cannot but honor and respect all of life.

Happiness Does Not Come from Externals

Dr. Henderson says,

"There's a knowing in your mind, and a knowing in your heart. If you know something in your heart, you'll do things differently. From the day I knew the truth, my whole life was different and I could see things differently. There was one day I was sitting in the 'C' cell lock-up, behind a thirty-foot wall in Atlanta. The cell just had a bunk bed and a toilet. At that time I took a count and I had thirteen things I could call my own, including my socks, the clothes I had on, a toothbrush, and my bible. That was quite a difference from a year before, when I had thousands and thousands of things, bank accounts and money, etc. And yet, I was as happy in that situation, in what people would call an intolerable, miserable situation, as I was before. In fact, I was happier. I learned that happiness does not come from externals, but from inside you, how you think about things. Happiness comes from wanting what you have, as opposed to trying to get what you don't have. When I had the presence of God with me, I could tolerate anything. Now, I don't see the point of living if you're not living for something.

"From that time on I have not deviated any in thoughts or deeds. I have a mission. I get up every day grateful that I have another day to accomplish it. I've gotten into writing and publishing and doing a radio show to share God's truths with the world."

In both Joel and Dr. Henderson's cases their spirituality is involved with the world, with relationships, and the mind, body, spirit connection. Their spirituality is manifested by helping others function in the highest manner possible for them.

Make a Distinction between
What Is Learned Behavior and What Is Innate

The experience of grace and peace that Dr. Henderson had is one that is searched for by many these days. Dr. Diane Shainberg, psychologist, and teacher of meditation says,

"There is a great deal of suffering both men and women go through, and right now many are turning to spirituality to deal with that pain. If you look at what men are really looking for, it is peace, coming to rest, finding comfort from within.

"Much of the pain we have is caused by the lies we tell. There are a great many things we hide. I think the tragedy of narcissm has a lot to do with not being able to be ourselves, not having our truth seen, heard, or honored. The question is, how much are we guided by the heart, and how much we have to pretend that we don't know how gorgeous, what a presence we all are?

"Many cannot do this because it was not appreciated, or validated when we were children. As a matter of fact, what we were taught in our families was not to be too gorgeous, brilliant, or too much of a presence. But there is an intelligence in us that leads us to something far beyond what we were allowed to say or be in our family, or conventional society."

The fact that we are all more, not less than what we think, is beautifully expressed by Henry Miller who says, "We have been destroying ourselves to adapt to an image, which has been nothing but a mirage. Nothing will liberate us but realization."

What is being described here is realization of the soul, divine spark, Buddha Nature within. Once we contact this aspect of our being, certain forms behavior are no longer possible for us, many lies and games become unnecessary.

"Men are so afraid that they're going to have their own personal truth taken away," says Dr. Shainberg. "Here's such a deep fear and hurt from the time they tried to be themselves and it didn't work out in their family that now they don't

know how to find comfort inside. Boys have this feeling they
have to be on their own, without the necessary ingredients,
which is a deep contact with their mothers and with their
own essence."

Dr. Shainberg is suggesting that without a deep primal contact
with the mother, a boy becomes adrift, disconnected from his
own ability to connect with his own essence and nurture himself. For some, a deep spiritual connection with God, or spirit,
actually can replace the missing bond with the mother. It is
another way to feel united with the universe, loved and at
home in the world. For others, although there has been a good
connection with the mother, the spiritual part of their nature,
remains dormant throughout life.

Living a Life that Is Unreal

"The mind is based upon scripts from the past," Dr. Shainberg said, "so they're not real in the present. Men who base
their lives upon these scripts, are always feeling fake, empty
and unreal. To be unreal is to be weak. But men are not
allowed to be weak, and can't show this weakness. So,
they're twice removed from what is really happening and
there is a deeper level of suffering because somehow it is a
disgrace. There is a terrible shame men feel that they will be
found out to be not just weak, but to be unreal, fraudulent."

Most men are not conscious of these feelings. What they
are conscious of are the symptoms which arise from it, depression, sorrow, disappointment and frustration. In order to
eradicate these symptoms completely, it is valuable to go to
the man's very sense of who he is and how he lives in the
world. Men who are presently engaged in spiritual practices

are attempting to do just that. They are working to place their lives upon a groundwork that is real and fulfilling.

So much energy is used in keeping false images of ourselves alive, and clinging to them. These false images live us, chew up our energy, take our life force. In a way they are dictators, constantly demanding that we behave in a way that may be against our grain. It's both a delight and relief in spiritual work when we let them go and begin to see that they are simply illusions, that we are all part of a greater whole, guided and cared for, all instruments of God.

Other therapists are also including the spiritual dimension in their work with clients. Armand DiMele, director of the DiMele Center for Psychotherapy, and host of the radio show *The Positive Mind* says,

> "I think this greater interest in spirituality we're seeing is part of the entire world's waking up," Mr. DiMele said. "It's everything, down to vegetarianism, alternative medicine, eliminating toxins. We are at the point now where we spend two dollars to drink a bottle of water, so, we're being forced to wake up to what's going on. The earth is crying out for it too."

Because of the damage done not only to our own bodies, minds and relationships, but to the very earth we live on, a new, larger perspective is needed to bring healing. This perspective must include spiritual principles, put into action. We have come to see that despite material progress, not including the spiritual in our lives has not brought the health, safety, kindness, or fulfillment all mankind yearn for.

"We'd better wake up because the pressures are enormous on everybody," said Mr. DiMele. "Women feel they've got to be thin, they're constantly worrying about gaining a pound and losing a pound, what they look like and whether they fit into a size 4 or 6. It's brutal. These days the package is all. And the package is a bizarre package too, it has little to do with who and what people really are inside.

"In order to sell a product you have to put it in very beautiful wrappings and box, so you can afford less for the product itself. Even if you buy chocolate candies for Valentine's Day, you buy a beautiful box, but inside you can put the junkiest chocolates and it doesn't matter, as long as you get the wrapping right. That's the way our lives have become, just getting the wrapping right, with junky chocolate inside. In fact, oftentimes, there's nothing in the box. There's so much emphasis upon the package that they forgot to put anything inside. There's no one home anymore.

"So, what spirituality really means," said Mr. DiMele, "is settling somewhere on the inside, alone, in this encapsulated ego."

By settling on the inside alone, Mr. DiMele is speaking of centering within, rather than receiving meaning and fulfillment from what we can receive from the outside world. This is a way of surrendering personal ego, turning to a different source for our happiness and security, rather than being at the mercy of the endless fluctuations of life.

Mr. DiMele is also making a wonderful distinction between being alone and feeling lonely. By settling on the inside alone, one realizes that when a person goes deep into aloneness, there is no loneliness anymore.

Mr. DiMele said,

"Loneliness is a feeling of discomfort with yourself. It has nothing to do with other people. People always feel lonely, if they don't like being with themselves. If you don't like you, you're going to be lonely. If you're not feeling happy with you, and want someone to fill up this missing spot, you'll feel lonely. No one can fill up the missing spot for you. Loneliness is always coming out of a missing connection with part of yourself."

Loneliness Doesn't Have to Do with Other People

"A giant step is recognizing that loneliness doesn't have to do with other people. You have to recognize the loneliness for what it is, and go through it. Spirituality isn't about feeling comfortable or running away. It's learning how to go through things that are real and true.

"In order to get into the space of aloneness rather than loneliness one has not to buy into the social messages of the society, and the illusory whirlwind that goes on."

Mr. DiMele maintains a connection with society.

"I'm willing to be a part of it, I'm not antagonistic to it, but I haven't swallowed all the values. The first step is to discard the wrong values. There's all kinds of junk that goes on in the mindstream that's very dangerous. For example, if I'm not married, I'll be half a person. If I don't have a lot of money, I'm not worth anything. I mean, come on. When you're in an environment with a strong belief system, it permeates you. You have to watch out for those concepts because they get in there and can be very destructive. Especially many of the men in the corporate world. They really define their worth by money, power, status in the company. The society at large is very influenced by these markers."

Again we see the extreme importance of stepping back and evaluating the effect of the values society has been presenting. Many lives are devoured by these values when the time hasn't been taken to carefully understand the impact they have, and what is true and what is not. This process of stepping back and evaluating can also be called contemplation, meditation, prayer, or growing up and assuming responsibility for who you are and what you believe. It is the heart and soul of all spiritual practice, and must be engaged in continually. As a man does this, he becomes more and more fulfilled.

> "This work is never complete," Mr. DiMele said. "You just make as much peace as you can everywhere. You can be a part of anything, but it doesn't have to be you. You don't have to run away from people, you've got to love people where they are—that's what the complete man can do. He can be with people without needing to change them.
>
> "I, personally, do this by not allowing myself the illusion that whatever is happening out there is real. I don't buy into all these endless crises in life. They look important, but by now I've learned that everything that looks critically important is not so important, and that everything will get solved in one way or another. I'm going to be a part of the solving, but I don't have to rush, to react, or get panicked about anything at all. Now if I don't have to bring panic to anything, it gives me so much more energy to just relax, and in the relaxed place I let it be, and solutions just come to me."

Find the Real World

"Look," Mr. DiMele continued, "the world we're living in is created by all the dreams of people and these dreams are keeping the world going. But there's a world that's real, in which you are connected to the entire universe. Find that real world."

This injunction to find the real world, or to find that which is real and meaningful to you, is the essence of all spiritual teachings. All teachings ask you to question the validity and truth of that which has seemed so solid and important, and to find that which will truly nourish and sustain you, no matter what is happening outside.

When the Real World Finds You

Not only does a man have to find the real world, but at certain moments the real world finds him, whether or not he is expecting it. Jacques Van Engel, an attractive man in his forties who works at the United Nations, has been deeply involved in a spiritual quest for many years. One day, an unexpected experience led him to a new exploration of himself.

"Spirituality has been extremely important to me since I was about twenty," he said. "Before that I was educated in a completely non-spiritual way. Religion was even frowned at in my family. We were more scientific-minded, only believing in what could be seen or heard. The objective of life, the biggest goal to be attained was some material comfort, which would then allow us to have some holidays, time off, swimming in the ocean."

The materialistic mode of life, in which only that which can be seen, touched, smelled, or heard, has value and reality—is a life devoid of spirituality. After all the pleasures have been experienced, and all the so-called success has been attained, it often wears thin.

"During my youth," Jacques said, "I had no experience of spirituality. My father's family was religious in the Jewish religion. Then, during the war my father's parents were exterminated, along with others in my family. After that my parents could not believe in God anymore, or in anything. In fact, spirituality was portrayed as something which didn't help humanity, because many religious people got killed anyway. So it all didn't make sense."

Many feel that the existence of God or Spirit is disproved by negative, unjust events that they have to undergo. They do not understand how God can allow such pain and suffering. The question of how God can allow this, must be explored deeply, as it is the very foundation of a truly spiritual life. This inability to find reconciliation arises from those who view God, or Spirit, as a beneficent parent, who must provide only pleasure and rewards to his children. It is a childlike viewpoint, self-involved point of view, where God exists simply to please us and fulfill our needs. This point of view does not ask what God requires of us, how we can fulfill His will and the needs of his creatures. It also does not address the deeper issue of why this suffering arises, and the many ways we can respond to it. Can we rise above our personal suffering? Can we grow sufficiently to be able to love no matter what goes on? Are we being taught and tested by all that comes our way?

Sudden Awakening

"When I was about twenty," Jacques continued, "I had a spiritual experience which changed my whole perspective on life. I was on a holiday in Devon, England, and I was in a serene environment, walking on the cliffs, when somehow the experience came to me. Suddenly my whole world was suddenly full of vibrations, full of joy. I was ecstatic, completely out of my normal, egoistic functioning. I think this experience is probably very close to what religious people experience when they pray to God. My experience was completely sudden and I didn't even know what was happening. I was in a receptive state, the world was perfect and complete. The experience ended after an hour or so and then I was back to my good, old self."

Jacques experienced what might be called a sudden enlightenment, or an experience of grace, of being allowed to participate in the vast, mysteriousness of the entire universe. He entered the world of bliss and joy.

"A few weeks later," Jacques continued, "I was back in Brussels, and met a Vedanta teacher, teaching non-duality. Somehow, I recognized that he was talking about the same thing that had happened to me. This is when my interest in spirituality, and my search started. It was like you taste something wonderful for the first time and you want to know what it was, and how to have it back again."

Jacques didn't experience a change in his quality of life right away. Some think that with one experience of enlightenment, grace, or God's presence, they are reborn and able to live in an entirely new way. This is rarely the case. The initial experience is an opening, an invitation. A great deal of work and purification must follow to integrate the experience, and those that follow it, into the marrow of one's everyday life.

Jacques said,

"After that experience the search to get back to that high was very long, it took years and years. First I listened to Vedanta teachers. Then my career evolved. I was sent to Asia and there I got into contact for the first time with Buddhism and Zen practice, where there is no talk anymore about things, just practice. It's like the difference is between reading how to ride a bicycle and doing it. When you hear about it, it's frightening, you fear you may fall from the bicycle. But when you just do it, and sit on the bike, that's another experience. And that's more what Zen practice was about. Doing without asking questions about it."

Jacques found that the actual practice of Zen, zazen, (Zen meditation), was a direct route to returning him to the original experience he had.

"When I came back to New York I got into a Zen practice here at the N.Y. Zendo with Eido Roshi," he continued, "and as I practiced more and more, that original experience became more prominent in my life. Now the biggest objective of my life is to find who I am, to find the here and now, to live in it. As this happens, I live more intensely. I listen to a concert more deeply, really see the colors of the trees when I walk. It used to be that when I went to a concert I would have so many daydreams of my own that I would hardly ever hear the music. I would be so full of my own thoughts that there would be no room for anything else."

Through his ongoing practice Jacques integrates his spirituality into everything, including his work.

"The job I have is seen as a means to live. I work so my spiritual search can continue, but not the other way around.

However, the practice does help a great deal at work as well. Often one gets interruptions, disturbances, negative comments from colleagues, and we start to fight. When we practice, we flow with it more, without fighting it. When the phone calls come, okay, it just comes. And when the colleague wants to talk to you, you're more open to it. You can hear the comments. No need to fight."

True Spirituality Is Not about Good and Bad

Many people think of spirituality as placing many restrictions upon them, or condemning various individuals, or groups, making life more constricted. There is the impression that if an individual becomes spiritual, he or she will begin to reject many aspects of life, to feel superior, even righteous.

"This is not at all true in Zen practice," Jacques said. "I think there are very few practices in the world where the accent is put on the light itself, or God itself, or Allah itself, or Christ or love itself, whatever the name. Most practices spend enormous amount of time battling each other that this is the truth, or that is the truth. They are focussed upon the form, not something else. In Zen the Master is pointing his finger to the moon. The disciple says 'What are you doing?' The Master slaps him and says, 'Don't get attached to my finger, what counts is the moon.'

"In the case of Zen, the focus is only on the moon, and not on the way you reach it. The accent is not on the forms, the way you behave. This is why I was so attracted to this particular practice. I always thought that other practices were more about good and bad, more about morality than about God. I came back to spirituality, but a spirituality that was devoid of moralistic, judgmental thoughts about who is evil and who is good."

Jacques has transcended what he sees as the negative aspects of spiritual experience, found the kernel of truth and goodness, and permitted himself to go forward despite painful experiences his family had in the past. In a sense, this can be seen as a healing for both Jacques and his family, a way of reopening the door to spirituality that makes it beautiful and real.

"When you get into real spirituality," he said, "when someone really finds the Oneness, usually that person becomes very kind, compassionate and open, because when you get to that realm of being, compassion comes up naturally. If you see someone else suffering, there's nothing else to do but to feel one with that person and offer help. But that help is a selfless help, not a dualistic kind."

Selfless Charity

By dualistic help, Jacques is referring to conditional help, help given to those considered worthy, or only to members of your own group. It also refers to all the honor and rewards people seek for giving charity. From the Zen point of view, that is not true giving at all, only self-aggrandizement.

"I think that when charity is practiced in a dualistic way often people have very good intentions to help others, but it often leads to catastrophe," Jacques said. "In non-dualistic approaches like Zen, other Buddhist streams and Vedanta, it is also recommended to help others, but without egoistic desire, to help all people, indiscriminately. The help includes being the other person, and feeling the love stream between you. That happens as we realize that all is one. That kind of help does real good. In fact then we can actually do as Christ advises, which is to pray for our enemies. We can easily do that because we see that there are no enemies. We are all one."

This point of view is coming from the very top of the mountain, where spirituality is seen as a means of uniting all people, judging none, simply extending an open hand. In order to do this, one must let go of attachment and preferences, seeing ourselves as belonging to the entire family on earth. In Zen practice attachment dissolves and one becomes free to truly see and be with whoever appears.

"What is very important," Jacques says, "is that one should not be attached to whatever group or practice we are in, feeling it is better than others. Because we are humans, attachments are dangerous. The real principle of Zen is that practice is a raft and the raft helps you cross the river, but once you cross the river, the raft should be discarded, meaning we should not cling to anything."

From this point of view spirituality is freedom, freedom to come and go, to love without strings, to give wholeheartedly, and to just be. This is not a flight from life, but an effort to free up one's original energies, and abilities and offer them to life, to contribute more fully. This form of spirituality allows an individual to experience all of life, be part of the world in a simple and healing manner. This is beautifully expressed in a quote by the great Zen Master Dogen:

"When he was completely enlightened he could walk through mud and be splashed with dirty water without being upset. He simply accepted mud as mud, and dirty water as dirty water. He was a free man, unattached to ideas of like or dislike. Such power comes from non-attachment."

True spirituality, whether it is expressed through Western or Eastern teachings and practices, are based upon the same truths of love, aliveness, hope, joy and gratitude for all that is constantly being given. It is based upon a recognition that we do not own this great world we are living in, but are here briefly to care for it, treasure each other, and utilize our time to leave light and warmth behind. Anything else is a distortion, and should be seen as such.

In closing, a quote from Bhagwan Rajneesh, spiritual teacher.

"Simply drop the effort to possess, to desire, to crave. When there is no craving, everything drops. You are simply in your purity. The moment craving is not there, the whole world becomes divine. It has always been so, only your eyes have not been open to see. Open eyes, unclouded by craving, the world and everything in it appears as the divine."

Touchstones to Remember

1. The search for deep roots and for our true nature brings meaning into our lives.

2. Spiritual practice is daily work. It happens slowly. Enjoy each step of the way.

3. The real fruits of practice can be seen in daily life, how a person treats others, including those he may not like.

4. Ego, a false sense of self and values, is the killer, not only of our life, but the lives of others.

5. If a man really believes he's a child of God, he knows he has his father's characteristics, that part of him is perfect, and he's worth loving and taking care of.

6. A man must know his mission, what God put him here to do. As soon as he starts doing it, his entire life will be wonderful.

7. There's so much emphasis upon the package these days, often there's nothing inside. A man must make sure he doesn't live his life this way. He must act from and honor who he truly is inside.

8. Being alone is not being lonely. In order to be spiritual one has to tolerate being alone, which means being who they are. When one lets the world become the world they become part of it. When they're opposing the world, it's no good.

9. Loneliness is a feeling of discomfort with oneself. It has nothing to do with other people. If a man doesn't like himself, he's going to be lonely.

10. Find the real world. That which is out there and looks so important is truly nothing at all. Discard wrong values, weed out and disengage from negative conditioning everyday.

11. No one is ever complete. They just make as much peace as they can. They must learn to love people where they are, to be with people without needing to change them.

12. Most important of all, don't be a hypocrite. Each person must walk their talk.

13. True spirituality allows a person to live more intensely, to be open, awake, and in touch with everything. It is not about judging who is good and who is bad.

14. A greater intelligence in us leads us to what we're allowed to know or say, that we're radiant beings, always in touch with God.

TEN

Getting Him to Talk

*"We but half express ourselves and are ashamed
of the divine idea which each of us represents."*
        —Ralph Waldo Emerson

Women complain they can't get men to talk. When the
time comes for intimate conversation, guys clam up,
offer a few, indecipherable grunts and expect women to magically understand what's going on. Women feel shut out, and
men feel misunderstood. Even in the best relationships, many
women feel a sense of loneliness so they turn to their girlfriends for intimate conversation. Unfortunately men often
have nowhere to turn. Without communication between partners, fault-finding and misunderstandings develop, and many
relationships turn sour.

However, there is something women don't realize. Men
want to talk—they desperately need to unburden themselves
and let the world know what's going on inside. Under the
right conditions, they'll talk all night long. In order to feel
healthy and alive, all human beings need to express what
they're thinking and feeling, need to be heard and responded
to, find out how they are being perceived.

Personal Inventory: Getting Him To Talk

Group A: Warriors, Heroes, Adventurers
Group B: Lovers, Dreamers, Peter Pans
Group C: Controllers, Perfectionists, Addicts
Group D: Wise Men, Gurus, Seers
Group E: A Real Guy!

SCORING
(Score each question from 1–4 in the following manner)

1. Not at all
2. Sometimes
3. Often
4. All the time

1. Does he answer with a grunt or two?

2. Does he give you long looks, pregnant with meaning?

3. Does he frequently bring up things you have told him in the past?

4. Does he hold grudges, way beyond the time the injury occurred?

5. Does he bring you little gifts, like chocolates, flowers and notes?

6. Is he always busy when you bring up a subject he doesn't like?

7. Does he spend a great deal of time comparing you to others?

8. Is he willing to sit down with you, put things aside, and talk?

9. Does he seem to know what you're thinking before you say a word?

10. Does he turn whatever you say into something much more complicated?

11. Does he want to know your secrets and what's happened in your day?

12. Is he always challenging you?

13. Does he speak to you physically, by being affectionate or making love?

14. Does he quote others when you're trying to work out something?

15. Is he forgiving, of himself and of you?

16. Has he already forgotten what the problem was about?

17. Is he willing to listen fully before saying anything?

18. Is he always talking about himself and what he's doing?

19. Does he immediately want to change the topic, play, or make love?

20. Can he easily put himself in your shoes?

ANSWERS

Group A: Warriors, Heroes, Adventurers
(Questions 6, 10, 12, 18) Score 12 or more

These men are usually "doers" not speakers. They enjoy great challenge and danger, and want to seize on a problem to work it out, not talk it to death. When time comes to talk to them, they're either busy, involved with their own projects, or use communication to complicate the matter or to challenge. The best way to get through to them is to meet them on their own turf. Present the issue as an adventure, something that will make them grow.

Group B: Lovers, Dreamers, Peter Pans
(Questions 2, 5, 13, 19) Score 12 or more

These men communicate in subtle and fanciful ways. They are involved with what is going on inside their dream world, and want to draw you into it as well. Many times these individuals expect that you will know what they are thinking and resent having to say it directly. They will frequently change the topic, or for an answer to a problem choose to show what they're feeling or thinking by physical means. The positive aspect of these men is that they are open to emotional intimacy, though not always expressed in mundane means, like words.

Group C: Controllers, Perfectionists, Addicts
(Questions 3, 4, 7, 11) Score 12 or more

These men use communication to control, threaten, compare or demean. They often bring up old wounds from the past, or compare you to others to make you shaky. Implicitly, they believe there is a certain way to be and specific answers they want to have. If you don't go along, there's trouble ahead.

When an individual is in this mode, it's important to be aware of what's going on and that true communication is not possible at this time. Bow out gracefully and come back later when they're more available.

Group D: Wise Men, Gurus and Seers
(Questions 9, 12, 14, 16) Score 12 or more

The wise men and gurus may be so involved with the larger meaning of life, so lost in their thoughts that it becomes difficult for them to come down to earth and take small, personal concerns seriously. They can make a person feel petty for caring about something as small as a pay check that's been lost, or a call they said they'd make, that never came. In order to communicate successfully here it's wise to frame your concerns as part of the big picture of life.

Group E: A Real Guy!
(Questions 8, 15, 17, 20) Score 12 or more

The real guys are available to sit down and listen, to hear, to talk. All that happens is of importance to them. Because they are free of the need to live according to an image and can be real, they are especially good at putting themselves into your shoes.

Trained for Silence

Most men have been taught it is unmanly to talk, to open up and tell all. They speak in code and believe that if they have to actually ask for what they want there is something wrong, that the women, or others in their lives, don't really know or care about them. Many men want to be magically understood without saying a word and believe this represents being loved. Wanting someone to anticipate our needs arises in childhood, when we expect our mother to hear our cries long before we utter them and be there with food the minute hunger arises, no questions asked.

Men are taught to present an invincible image to the world. As children boys are told, *"Boys don't cry. That stuff's for girls."* Of course implicit in the idea is that expressing feelings represents weakness, something for girls, not boys. They are also taught that strength comes from not being needy, that it is preferable to be the strong, silent type. In addition, withholding communication can also represent power and control. It is as if they say, "I'm powerful, I need nothing from you."

For many men, as they grow into maturity, the idea of "talking" or expressing themselves openly become alien and dangerous. Communication represents vulnerability and triggers the fear that they may be acting like "girls." When their wives or girlfriends then ask them to be intimate, to talk openly, or share feelings, men feel as though they are in a double bind. Part of him wants to talk, another part wants to be seen as strong. Deep within they may be yearning to get closer, at the same time they may fear losing themselves.

Irresponsible Communication

"If she knows too much about me, I'll be putty in her hands," said Robert, a thirty-year-old executive. "I never let a woman know what's really doing inside. Why should I? She'll only throw it back at you when there's a fight later."

Robert lives expecting trouble. In fact, he not only looks

forward to it, but does his share to quietly make it happen. It's the way he releases his pent-up feelings.

"It's okay to fight," Robert continued. "You get closer later. I mean, if you can survive a good fight, then the two of you have a chance."

Robert replaces open communication—and the intimacy it provides—with fights. He grew up in a home where he watched his parents fight constantly, rebuking each other and the children. Each engaged in irresponsible communication and expressed their anger and frustration by projecting it outside and blaming the world, not taking responsibility for their own feelings. The release this behavior brings is at best temporary, and further negative consequences always follow. Fighting in this way is a substitute for true communication and closeness.

"Once you fight it out," Robert continued, "then you know who's who, and where each of you belong. The winner is top dog, and the loser is more careful after that." For Robert, communication, via fighting, is for the purpose of establishing rank. Who will be in control of the relationship? This is not communication, but sparring. It is domination, masking itself as friendship or love.

Real communication is never about establishing who's on top and who's below. It's not about winning or losing. The essence of real communication is always about love.

Popular wisdom has it that most men would rather spar than talk—that they want to be constantly in control. Nothing can be further from the truth. In fact, the price a man pays for withholding and sparring is the constant strain of not being known and living a false self. He is not ever really heard and also does not hear, making him feel alienated and alone. Love relationships, which allow us to bridge the gap between ourselves and others, then become a place for more hiding, sparring and disconnection.

Communication is a massive topic. Basically, there is nothing but communication streaming around us, yet most of us hear only static and noise, without and within. The volume and mass of communication can become overwhelming so that we tune it out. Unfortunately, we also tune out the communication that comes from within. Rather than opening ourselves to communication, we shut it out.

But as we close off to the outside world, not only do we misunderstand what is happening around us, we feel separate from others, and the state of loneliness this produces induces depression, anger, and all forms of addiction. In order to set things right, we need to learn not only how to speak, but to hear what is going on with others, as well as what is going on with ourselves. When we stop labeling and judging each other, the possibility of true communication begins. As we allow ourselves to receive and offer true communication, loneliness, confusion and even illness often subsides.

> "I can't really talk to her," Robert says, "because whatever I say I know she's judging me. She's comparing me to other guys she's been with, or figuring how she can change my mind. Sure, sometimes the whole thing's exhausting." When it reaches that point, Robert says, "I just go with the fellas to the ballgame."

What Is Communication?

"There are no gifted and ungifted here—only those who give themselves, and those who withhold."
                                                                —*Martin Buber*

What is communication? Why is it easy to open up around some, while around others we go into a shell? Communication exists on many levels—verbal, physical, intuitive. We receive many messages unconsciously and often respond to them.

Conventional wisdom says we'll like and feel comfortable with someone because of his good qualities and dislike or feel uneasy around someone because of his faults. But it often doesn't work that way. Sometimes we love the so-called villains and don't really feel so good around the so-called saints. No matter what words are spoken, we respond to something deeper—to the non-verbal messages being given and received and our inner sense of what's being truly said and what we expect to hear in return.

Families have their own intricate ways of communicating with each other. Some dedicate all their efforts to dissembling—keeping each other from knowing the truth. There are as many different ways of communicating as there are people, and just as many different ways of listening or being heard. Some lives are dedicated to not communicating, but engaging in deception—hiding, withholding and presenting a front. These individuals live in a prison of their own making. However, their unwillingness to communicate is also a form of communication.

All pretenses are eventually transparent. No matter how much we play act with one another, our deeper communications are always being heard. And they are always being responded to.

Ed Pankau, nationally acclaimed private investigator, and best-selling author of *How to Hide Your Assets and Disappear*, deals constantly with communication in the lives of his clients and himself. He says that in order to get a guy to reveal himself, "First you've got to get his confidence. He's got to feel he's not going to be rejected. There's got to be a level of trust there, so he can open up. The other way to get him to talk is when there's fear. He gets scared that if he doesn't open up and confess, he's going to lose everything."

Communication that is based on fear is short-lived, at best, and directed toward protecting what a person has. It certainly is not the kind of communication that builds a healthy life or relationship.

How to Help Him Feel Safe and Confident

It's not so hard to help a man feeling safe so he can communicate easily. Mr. Pankau said,

> "Well, listen to what he is saying, and beyond listening, offer something positive in return. After he tells you some things you could then say, 'Well, that's not so bad. I've done worse.' Or, 'That's happened. It's done, it's over. Where do we go from here?' Let him know you're on his team, and not sitting there judging him."

The sense that a man is being judged is the single greatest block to his communication. He may already be judging himself, so if he feels a critical atmosphere from the other person, nothing can develop. He'll watch every word, censor himself and not open up.

Mr. Pankau dismisses the myth that men don't like to talk with,

> "Nonsense. A lot of them need to and like to, but there's an approach–avoidance syndrome, because they're afraid if they do open up, someone's going to laugh at them and if someone does laugh, they're humiliated. They're afraid of the rejection. Men are much more afraid of rejection than women,

by the way. People don't realize that. You've got to start out
your communication realizing that. What you have to do is
to create a level of communication that makes a guy feel
confident. Give up a little something of yourself first, so it's
not just him exposing himself. Then he'll think, well, she's
doing it too, I'm not alone in this, she must really understand
what's going on."

In order for there to be mutual communication, there must
be mutual disclosure between the partners. A person must feel,
we're in this together, and that feeling itself allows him to
feel safe and able to go further.

"Everybody has problems, fears and skeletons in the closet.
Many guys feel, 'if I reveal this, she'll leave me.' You have
to show that this is not the case. One of the ways to do that
is to reveal something about yourself that shows that you
have to have as much trust in them as they have in you.
Trust is a two-way street. You can't have any communication
without trust. That's the first step."

Trust is a crucial ingredient of all relationships, but especially when it comes to communication. If an individual feels
his communication will be distorted, misunderstood, told to
others, or thrown back at him at a later date, it is impossible
for him to feel safe and open. These factors have to be clearly
established right up front. Some people hoard confidences to
use against the person at a later time. This pattern is poison
in a relationship. It is also crucial to remember that what was
communicated at one point in time may not be the way a man
feels later. Feelings and perceptions change—allowance must
be made for that. Some people, however, hold onto what has
been said at one point in time, and never let it go. The ability

to forgive may be just as simple as realizing that what was true a year ago, may not be true now. True communication requires the ability to remain in the present moment, available to what is now happening, and to let the past be over when it's done.

"As a detective," said Mr. Pankau, "I see lots of people who have problems in the sexual area, where communication and trust are so important. I hear all kinds of stories. People don't become fulfilled because they don't communicate. And the same thing goes from an emotional standpoint. People don't take the time to know what the other person needs or wants.

"Many men might, in fact, be ashamed to communicate about such intimate details as their sexual or emotional need," Mr. Pankau said, "They've got to be a macho man. There's no school to go to learn how to be a good talker, a good listener, or a good lover. People learn how to deal with this by experimenting on their own. There are a lot of life skills that people just aren't getting. It amazes me—like the real basic ones of talking and listening."

The Illusion of Communication

*"Forty-nine years,
And not a word said."*
—Buddha

As we spend our days talking and listening many of us feel we're hearing what the other is saying and making ourselves known. Nothing could be farther from the truth. Many speak to fill up empty space, or to make themselves feel smart. Some speak to play the role of authority, others to dominate. Some speak to block out communication, to distract from what is really happening, or to manipulate, to get what they want for themselves, or change the other's point of view. Some speak to attack, belittle or flatter. Others simply speak for the pleasure of being heard, of having someone pay attention.

Listening can be distorted as well. While seeming to listen, many are busy preparing the answers in their minds, or just waiting for the other to be finished, or calculating what the person is really saying, judging what will happen down the road. This has nothing to do with listening. In order to really listen, one must learn to be open and still. Silence is the ingredient needed, silence within and silence without. We must learn to make a space for another. Real listening requires curiosity and courage—the courage to be present and available, the curiosity to discover what's being said.

There is a story told about Martin Buber, the great philosopher, professor and theologian. He was once visited in his office at the university by a student who came to speak with him about difficulties he was having. Mr. Buber set the time aside and put his work down when the student came in. The student spoke, and Mr. Buber listened, or so he thought. He said a few things to the student and after the interview, the young man left and Mr. Buber resumed his work. A little later on he learned that the young man went home from the interview and killed himself.

This event changed Mr. Buber's life. He realized that, although he had listened to what the young man said, he hadn't really heard a thing. He'd heard only the words, but the need behind it, the real communication had gone unperceived.

Mr. Buber then put his work aside and day and night asked himself one question only: What is it that another seeks when he comes to a person in a state of desperation? The answer he finally found was that the young man sought a Presence through which he could feel that there was still meaning.

How is this Presence cultivated? How do we create an environment in which the deeper parts of a person are free to speak out?

Some Who Feel They Are Able to Talk Easily

Lewis Harrison, Healer and Director of the Academy of Natural Healing, tall, jovial and naturally expressive, has a different experience regarding communication.

"As far as I'm concerned," he said, "I, personally, tell everybody everything. I can't hold it back if I want to." He grinned. "My wife is willing to listen to everything. I don't have to lie to her at all."

Not only is Lewis's wife willing to hear what he says, but she is willing to take action to give him what he asks for. This is communication taken to the highest level. Her ability to understand was manifested both in words and in deeds.

"The way I am now goes back to my life prior to my marriage," Lewis said. "I never censored myself around women and always had the most grief around women I had to censor myself around. My wife trusts me implicitly. I don't give her anything to distrust me by, though I'm sure other women would see some of the things I do as warning signs. For instance, I'm a flirt, but I'm monogamous. My wife knows and trusts that, therefore I can communicate all my feelings to her about others, and explore the whole issue any time I want. I'm not comfortable with lying. We all want love and we want to give love but are not willing to do what is required to make that happen, and part of that is honesty from other people about how they are."

Being Willing to Accept What the Other Has to Say

In order to communicate so honestly, you have to accept honesty from others, and many people won't. Perhaps that's why they won't even be honest with themselves.

Mr. Harrison said,

"That's key with me. I am willing to listen to and accept whatever it is my wife or anyone has to say. I just do it. For example, once my wife and I were in Fire Island at the beach and I'm looking at her, and it's not a really romantic moment. What happened was she was actually unattractive to me right then, but the relationship was in a very strong space. So what was going through my mind was the things about her I didn't like. As a result of that thought I said to her, 'Is there anything about me you really don't like?' "

This is an example of taking radical responsibility for feelings. Rather than project his negativity, and tell his wife what he didn't like about her, Mr. Harrison saw this as an opportunity to work with a concept called *mirror-image*. This concept says that what you perceive in the outside world, you are truly perceiving about yourself. What you dislike about another, is a reflection of what you do not like about yourself. Robert Bly calls this *projecting the shadow*. We are projecting our own self-rejection and hatred upon someone outside. Mr. Harrison took a courageous action by reversing this process, by asking his wife to tell him what she didn't like about him.

"The wife said, 'Well, you're okay.' "

He continued.

"I said, 'I know I'm okay, but are there things you really don't like? Why don't you tell me all of them?' She said,

'That's not really necessary,' but finally listed about forty things. Not only were they awful, but they were accurate. They were all things I didn't like either. I was grateful then for her willingness to be with someone like me. It made me humble. I thought, I would never be with someone like that."

Surrender Self-Aggrandizement

This process is a beautiful description of willingness to surrender a false sense of one's self-importance and-aggrandizement, and be present for the truth between two people. It is rare to see it in action in this way. Lewis truly wanted to hear the truth from his partner, and was open to her experience at that moment. By finding the similarities between them, he didn't have to put blame or aversion on her.

From a psychological point of view, it might be said, hearing her criticisms of him made him feel less guilty about his negative thoughts about her. It also confirmed for him the feeling that he was fortunate to be with her at all. The larger point is that in all relationships, both positive and negative feelings about the other fluctuate regularly. When we start to see the negative about the other, it can be chastening to remember there are also negative qualities about ourselves. This is a form of humility and self-clarification, one of the highest outcomes of all relationships.

Mostly, we only want to hear the positive—that is, hear only half the truth. If we can be open to receiving and sharing the full picture, then, through this act of communication and acceptance, our shame, fear and negative feelings can subside. We can get a whole sense of ourselves and possibly correct parts we may not like. At times we can even become humble, as Lewis said, and not have to live out a false image and inner demand of perfection.

When It's Appropriate to Hold Back

Some believe it is appropriate to "lie" or to withhold the bare truth.

"In some cases, with some men, I think it may be more important for women to be kind than truthful. You've got to know who you're with. It's hard for most men to take the truth. I'm different, but most men are pretty fragile," Lewis said.

"Even where my wife is concerned, I don't really tell her *everything*. There are certain areas of life where I feel that she psychologically behaves in ways that are less than she's capable of, and I don't tell her that. And there are things about herself that really can't be changed. So I lie. I tell her that they're fine. In the interest of kindness and her feeling better about herself. These are things that couldn't be changed without being dishonest to herself. She could change it, but then she'd be living a lie."

Now we are looking at the overall purpose of the communication—what the effect will be of saying every little thing. If the intent is beneficial, not to abuse or harm, that intention itself will censor certain communications, or couch issues in ways in which they can be absorbed and readily heard.

The Neuro Linguistic Programming (NLP) teachings say that you can know the intent of your communication by the response you receive. Communications can be made in many ways, using many types of words, tones, inflections and body language. You can say "I love you," with mocking contempt in your voice and the person will recoil from you. You can say "Get out of here," with so much warmth and love that the person will come closer. We communicate only a portion of our message with the words we choose.

What is it you are truly saying? What is the message behind the words? Are you wanting to draw the person close, or reject them? Do you want them to feel lesser than you, or feel good? The answer is found internally and stems from what is happening with you at the time.

How Many Can Really Have Honest Relationships?

Armand DiMele, Director and Founder of the DiMele Center for Psychotherapy and the host of the *Positive Mind* show said,

"In discussing the question of honest communication, is it even possible to have honest relationships? The assumption is everybody's going to be honest. The truth is—nobody is. Or very few people are.

"Now there are two reasons that people are not honest. One is—the consequences are too big. If you're honest about certain things, if you tell your wife you had a flirtation with your secretary in the office and you were fooling around, playing with each other, it's going to create a tremendous amount of problems. So, one thing for sure, you can't be honest if the other person is not going to celebrate the honesty. Honesty is something to celebrate rather than squelch."

Celebrating Honesty

Mr. DiMele says there are women who can celebrate honesty. He said,

"I know women who can. I know women who could say, 'you know honey, I could fully understand your playing around with that woman because you're such a passionate guy, but if you go further than that, it would really disturb me.' There are women who say 'I value the honesty so much that I want you to be who you are, and I want to know who you are, and if that's who you are, I want to at least see it.' It's a problem. Do we really want to see who our mate is?"

T. S. Eliot, the poet, has said that "Humankind cannot bear very much reality." This points to the fact that certain truths cannot be accepted or absorbed so easily. Too much reality can shock deeply, and an individual must be prepared for it. Our defenses exist to protect us from that which we cannot tolerate. One may say that the process of growth in an individual is the process of being able to receive and accept more and more of life as it truly is.

"Women—and men too—can feel crushed about a lot of things," said Mr. DiMele. "What men and women seem to want is to have the person who they think they should have. They keep that person in a fantasy and implicity are saying, 'please don't break my fantasy. Don't tell me about anything that changes my idea of who you are.' The two people live in neutral corners and know little about each other. This produces normal estrangement which most people live with."

Mr. DiMele is suggesting that honesty is not always highly valued in a relationship. Some may prefer to keep up the fantasy they have been living with. Others want the comfort that small lies can bring. Some have no idea at all how to even begin being honest, or what the rewards of that would be.

The natural process of bonding, deepening a relationship

and growing together includes revealing oneself more and more truthfully, and being willing to accept the other's truth and revelation as well. This is a process which goes on over time. When both partners are willing to engage in it, there is no end to the heights that the relationship can grow.

An Invitation to Be Honest

"If you want someone to talk, you have to extend an invitation," Mr. DiMele says, "state it as a preference. You might prefer that the person be honest with you, but it can't be a demand. An emotionally backed demand doesn't work. Ken Keyes talked about it. This means I can't demand any particular communication from you. If I'm asking you a question—but sitting on a mine-field ready to explode if you don't give me the answer I want—no man will be honest, because he doesn't want to be bothered with the explosion.

"You've also got to be smart and realize when a discussion is going nowhere, when no matter how hard you try, it's not going to work too. When you're in an argument with someone and everything you say is countered by the other person, that's not honest communication. It's stonewalling, and it's better to stop right then.

"It is important to realize what is going on and not engage in destructive games. Focus upon the intention behind the words. Respond to the intention, not simply to the words that are being said. When a person is open to true give and take is the best time to embark upon real conversation."

There are times when we are naturally more open to others, and times when we are preoccupied, either with tasks to be done, or other worries and concerns. To simply realize and acknowledge the power of proper timing is an enormous help.

To know that no one person is always available for us saves a great deal of grief. To simply say, "This is not the right time to talk about this. Let's try later," and to respect that necessity, can forestall a great deal of conflict and failed attempts at communication.

"There's never a way to get him to talk—only a way to extend an invitation and then setting a fertile ground," DiMele says. "And remember, if he's not honest with you, it's possible you have made it unsafe for him. This is not about blaming—but realizing the responsibility of both individuals to create an environment that is safe, and nonjudgmental, where communication has a place to live."

The Present of Honesty

"So, if a woman can say to a man, 'I thank you for giving me this present of honesty,' that would be such a wonderful thing. I do it with the people who work for me. I say, 'it's the biggest complement to me that you care enough about me that you want to bring this communication, including your anger to me.'

"If one can realize that the entire range of feelings—love, anger, sorrow, joy—all are gifts when honestly communicated, that itself would turn everything around. Whenever a person is truly communicating they are giving a part of themselves.

"What many therapists do," Mr. DiMele said, "is tend to idealize a perfect state, create something that does not exist. What I do is make it all okay. Let's say you are the kind of guy who's afraid to talk to anybody, let's say you're the kind of woman who's always angry—fine. What I do is ask, how do we now find the love that's in the middle of this? *Can*

we love each other with all our fears and lies? How do we
dance with all our broken wings?"

This question is deeply in keeping with the Zen point of
view, where the totality of the person is always accepted just
as they are in this moment. And then again in the next moment. For love to be vital and real, it must happen admist all
the broken pieces of our lives. All the ideals and images we
create of how things have to be, are illusions and distract our
attention from the perfection of what is right before our eyes.

Don't Fix Me—Don't Change Me

"When you start picking away at all the broken wings, it's
endless and the person hates themselves all the more," Mr.
DiMele continued. "So maybe what he needs to say is 'Leave
it alone. This is the best I got. Don't fix me. Don't change
me. I don't want to feel that I'm under some scrutiny to
change. I may change if I feel in some way accepted. And
if I've got some behavior that's rubbing against you in such
a wrong way, you must oppose me. I don't ask you to go
along with all the parts of me. But don't blame *me*—don't
make it that *I* am wrong. Take responsibility for the communication. Tell me how *you* feel about it."

Men are asking for respect and acceptance for who they
are right now, not for some image or need a woman wants
them to fulfill. The pressure to change and improve, makes a
man feel as though he is not good enough, not essentially
loveable.

"Men are filled with so many demands to be all things to
all people, they don't know what to say to who. We must
learn simple acceptance of who a man is—this entails giving

up your own fantasies and expectations of him, and allowing him to be who he is. This entails the process of revelation— *letting him be revealed,* both to himself and to you."

We feel compelled to hide and disguise the parts of ourselves that are considered unacceptable. However, these parts that are hidden smolder and create problems of all kinds. They need to see the light of day, to be heard, expressed and understood. Once this happens, that which is truly undesirable often fades away, no longer drains the person, and more self-respect and self-understanding are attained.

Preparing for a Real Meeting

Communication between two people can be seen as a preparatory step for the next level, which is a real meeting, an encounter so deep that it is healing and puts us in touch not only with the other person, but with that which is greater than us all.

During this kind of encounter we simply become fully available. We are present not only to the other, but to all of life. It is during these moments that the fulfillment of all our yearnings are realized and true oneness is attained. A wonderful poem by an eleven-year-old boy, Peter Rosengarden, says it beautifully:

Stopping,
and counting every sound,
stopping
and seeing every stone,
stopping,
and letting in the wind,
stopping,
and not having to be somebody.

Bhagwan Shree Rajneesh, the great teacher of meditation and religion, said of communication:

"Really, only through silence is one related. And if you know the language of silence then you can be related to anything, because rocks are silent, trees are silent, the sky is silent. Everything exists in silence. If a rock is there in your hand, the rock is not chattering within itself and you are chattering. That's why you cannot be related to the rock. The rock is open, vulnerable, inviting. The rock will welcome you, but your chattering becomes the barrier. Even with human beings you cannot be in deep relationship for this reason, there can be no intimacy.

"When you are silent, open, ready to meet and welcome, you will never say that no one loves you, and you will never feel it. Now, you pretend that someone loves you, but deep down you know. Even lovers go on asking each other, 'Do you love me?' Everyone is afraid, uncertain, insecure, and they can never be certain. The lover can say, 'Yes, I love you,' but it never gives any guarantee. Only in deep silence are all questions answered, is love secure."

Touchstones to Remember

1. Beneath our words, our body language, our subtle movements and messages say much more. What is your facial expression saying? How about your tone of voice? Know your intention in the communication.

2. Make it safe for the person to express what he's feeling. Don't sit in judgment, but share some of your

similar experiences, so he knows he's not in this alone.

3. Know the right time for communication. If the person is being irrational or stubborn, unable to hear at that moment, call it quits and take a walk around the block.

4. Listen without demanding a certain response. Give the other the freedom to express what's in his heart.

5. Don't Fix Him—Don't Change Him. Let him be who he is and make it all right.

6. Learn how to listen, to become empty and still, providing a presence and the willingness to know what he thinks.

7. Celebrate honesty. Realize that whatever is being communicated truthfully is the gift of himself.

"Just as the most eager speaking at one another does not make for a conversation, so for true communication, no sound is necessary, not even a gesture."
—*Martin Buber*

RESOURCES

Dr. Robert J. Berk, psychoanalyst, psychotherapist, training analyst. Postgraduate Center for Mental Health. 155 East 76 Street, New York, NY 10021, (212) 744-5716.

Ernest Castaldo, Teacher, Sedona Releasing Method, Voice Coach, (212) 863-7990.

Armand DiMele, Director and Founder DiMele Center for Psychotherapy, host, radio show, "The Positive Mind," (WBAI). 119 West 57 Street, New York, NY 10019. (212) 757-4488.

Dr. Dan Foley, licensed insurance broker and registered representative of the National Association of Security Dealers, with 20 years of experience. (646) 227-8754.

Rabbi Joseph Gelberman, Interfaith Rabbi, Founder New Seminary. (212) 866-3795.

Lewis Harrison, Director, Academy of Natural Healing, consulting, relationship coach. 40 West 72nd Street, New York, N.Y. 10024. (212) 724-8782.

Dr. R. Winn Henderson is a retired medical doctor, author of nine books including *The Cure of Addiction, The 12 Steps, Doctors Don't Lie, The Four Questions, Share Your Missions* and others. He is producer and host of the internationally syndicated radio talk show "Share Your Mission," director of The Recovery Group, founder of The Destiny House, a public speaker and seminar leader, and the inventor of the HCSS medical treatment for Psoriasis. Web site *www.intl-speakers-network.com/rwhenderson* or http://user.icx.net/~drhenderson. E-mail:drhenderson@icx.net. Mail: 4301 Washington Pike, Knoxville, Tennessee, 37917. Phone: (865) 546-5537 (voice or fax). For a detailed explanation of Dr. Henderson's ordeal and transformation send an E-mail with "What Happened" on the subject line.

Mr. Thom Lisk, Professional Speakers Bureau, 112 Firth Avenue, Worthington, OH 43085. (614) 841-1776.

Lt. General Anthony Lukeman, (703) 743-5081, *Lukemans @aol.com*. Children's poetry.

Leslie Malin, MSW. Executive Coaching, President, Management by Design, Career Transition Coaching. (516) 671-5662.

Dr. Selwyn Mills, psychotherapist, Gestalt therapist, men's groups. 90 Schenck Avenue, Great Neck, New York 11021. (516) 829-9739.

Edmund J. Pankau, Private Investigator, Best-Selling Author, *Hide Your Assets and Disappear* and *Check It Out—Everyone's Guide To Investigation*. (713) 224-3777. Ejp@pankau.com.

Howard Rossen, MSW, psychotherapist, gay and straight, private practice. 59 West 74 Street, New York, N.Y. 10023. (212) 877-6069.

Bill Solomon, Avatar Master/Wizard. Create The Reality You Prefer. (212) 297-0933, solomonomolos@cs.com.

Joel Slavis, President Lightwave Concept. (212) 677-5267.

SELECTED BIBLIOGRAPHY

A Little Book on the Human Shadow, **Robert Bly** (HarperSan-Francisco)

The Art Of Loving, **Erich Fromm** (Harper and Row)

He, Revised Edition, **Robert Johnson** (Harper and Row)

C. G. Jung, Symbols of Transformation, **Carl Jung** (Princeton University Press)

The Light of Discovery, **Toni Packer** (Tuttle Publishing)

The Book of the Secrets (Volume IV), **Bhagwan Shree Rajneesh** (Rajneesh Foundation)